Mathcounts Tips for Beginners

Annie Zhao

http://www.mymathcounts.com/index.php

ABOUT THE BOOK:

This book teaches you some important math tips that are very effective in solving many Mathcounts problems. It is for students who are new to Mathcounts competitions but can certainly benefit students who compete at state and national levels.

Contributors

Yongcheng Chen, Ph.D., Author.
Jane Chen, Author.
Guiling Chen, Owner, mymathcounts.com, Typesetter, Editor .

ISBN-13: 978-1470050931
ISBN-10: 1470050935

Please contact us at mymathcounts@gmail.com for suggestions, corrections, or clarifications.

Table of Contents

Example 1: I have a frog who hops stairs either one or two steps at a time. Our staircase has 11 steps. How many different ways can the frog hop the stairs?

Solution: 144.

The frog has one way to hop up to stair 1.

It has two ways to hop up to stair 2 (it can hop one stair at a time twice or it can hop two stairs at a time).

The frog has three ways to hop up to stair 3 (it can hop one stair at a time three times, $1 + 1 + 1$; or it can hop one stair first then hop two stairs at a time, $1 + 2$; or it can hop two stairs at a time first then hop one stair, $2 + 1$).

The pattern is as follows:

Stairs	Number of ways	Note
6	13	$(5 + 8 = 13)$
5	8	$(3 + 5 = 8)$
4	5	$(2 + 3 = 5)$
3	3	$(1 + 1 + 1, 1 + 2,$ and $2 + 1)$
2	2	$(1 + 1,$ and $2)$
1	1	1

Please note that this is the Fibonacci numbers:

Stairs:	1	2	3	4	5	6	7	8	9	10	11
Ways:	1	2	3	5	8	13	21	34	55	89	**144.**

GENERAL CASE:

N_1 means that the number of ways the frog can hop up to the stair 1
N_2 means that the number of ways the frog can hop up to the stair 2
N_3 means that the number of ways the frog can hop up to the stair 3
N_4 means that the number of ways the frog can hop up to the stair 4
N_5 means that the number of ways the frog can hop up to the stair 5
N_6 means that the number of ways the frog can hop up to the stair 6.

<u>**Case 1:**</u> The frog can hop 1 stair or 2 stairs at a time
We need to get N_1 and N_2. We call them "the initial conditions". $N_1 = 1$, and $N_2 = 2$.

With N_1 and N_2, we are able to calculate any term:
$N_3 = N_2 + N_1$.
$N_4 = N_3 + N_2$.
. . . .

<u>**Case 2:**</u> The frog can hop 1, 2, or 3 stairs at a time.

We need to get N_1, N_2 and N_3. $N_1 = 1$, $N_2 = 2$, and $N_3 = 4$.

With N_1, N_2 and N_3, we are able to calculate any term:
$N_4 = N_3 + N_2 + N_1$.
$N_5 = N_4 + N_3 + N_2$.
$N_6 = N_5 + N_4 + N_3$.
. . . .

<u>**Case 3:**</u> The frog can hop 1, 2, 3, or 4 stairs at a time.

We need to get N_1, N_2, N_3, and N_4. $N_1 = 1$, $N_2 = 2$, $N_3 = 4$, and $N_4 = 8$.

With N_1, N_2, N_3, and N_4, we are able to calculate any term:
$N_5 = N_4 + N_3 + N_2 + N_1$
$N_6 = N_5 + N_4 + N_3 + N_2$
. . . .

<u>**Case 4:**</u> The frog can hop 1, or 3 stairs at a time.

We see that the order of 1, 2, 3 is interrupted: 1, $\boxed{2}$, 3.

We still need to get N_1, N_2, and N_3. But we notice that $\boxed{2}$ is missing. $N_1 = 1$, $N_2 = 1$, and $N_3 = 2$.

With N_1, N_2, and N_3, we are able to calculate any term with a little modification of the case 2:

$N_4 = N_3 + \boxed{N_2} + N_1 = N_3 + N_1$

$N_5 = N_4 + \boxed{N_3} + N_2 = N_4 + N_2$

. . . .

Case 5: The frog can hop 2, or 3 stairs at a time.

We see that the order of 1, 2, 3 is interrupted: $\boxed{1}$ 2, 3.

We still need to get N_1, N_2 , and N_3. But we notice that $\boxed{1}$ is missing. $N_1 = 0$, $N_2 = 1$, and $N_3 = 1$.

With N_1, N_2, and N_3, we are able to calculate any term with a little modification of the case 2:

$N_4 = \boxed{N_3} + N_2 + N_1 = N_2 + N_1$

$N_5 = \boxed{N_4} + N_3 + N_2 = N_3 + N_2$

. . . .

Case 6: The frog can hop 1, or 4 stairs at a time.

We see that the order of 1, 2, 3, 4 is interrupted: 1, $\boxed{2}$, $\boxed{3}$, 4.

We still need to get N_1, N_2, N_3. and N_4. But we notice that $\boxed{2}$ and $\boxed{3}$ are missing. $N_1 = 1$, $N_2 = 1$, $N_3 = 1$, and $N_4 = 2$.

With N_1, N_2, N_3. and N_4, we are able to calculate any term with a little modification of the case 3:

$N_5 = N_4 + \boxed{N_3} + \boxed{N_2} + N_1 = N_4 + N_1$

$N_6 = N_5 + \boxed{N_4} + \boxed{N_3} + N_2 = N_5 + N_2$

. . . .

Use the method outlined here you are able to generate as many cases as you like. We just summarize 11 commonly used cases below:

CASES COMMONLY USED:

Stairs hopped	Forms	Number of ways	Cases
1, 2	(1. 2)	$N_3 = N_2 + N_1$	(1)
1, 2, 3	(1, 2, 3)	$N_4 = N_3 + N_2 + N_1$	(2)
1, 2, 3, 4	(1, 2, 3, 4)	$N_5 = N_4 + N_3 + N_2 + N_1$	(3)
1, 3	(1, □, 3)	$N_4 = N_3 + 0 + N_1 = N_3 + N_1$	(4)
2, 3	(□, 2, 3)	$N_4 = 0 + N_2 + N_1 = N_2 + N_1$	(5)
1, 4	(1, □, □, 4)	$N_5 = N_4 + 0 + 0 + N_1 = N_4 + N_1$	(6)
2, 4	(□, 2, □, 4)	$N_5 = 0 + N_3 + 0 + N_1 = N_3 + N_1$	(7)
3, 4	(□, □, 3, 4)	$N_5 = 0 + 0 + N_2 + N_1 = N_2 + N_1$	(8)
1, 2, 4	(1 2, □, 4)	$N_5 = N_4 + N_3 + 0 + N_1 = N_4 + N_3 + N_1$	(9)
1, 3, 4	(1, □, 3, 4)	$N_5 = N_4 + 0 + N_2 + N_1 = N_4 + N_2 + N_1$	(10)
2, 3, 4	(□, 2, 3, 4)	$N_5 = 0 + N_3 + N_2 + N_1 = N_3 + N_2 + N_1$	(11)

Example 2: I have a pet cat Tiger who climbs stairs either one or three steps at a time. Our staircase has 11 steps. How many different ways can Tiger climb the stairs?

Solution: 41.

This is the case 4. We still need to get N_1, N_2, and N_3. $N_4 = N_3 + N_1$.
Tiger has one way to climb stair 1, 1 way to climb stair 2, and 2 ways to climb stair 3 (1 + 1 + 1, and 3).
With the formula $N_4 = N_3 + N_1$, the sequence is as follows: 1, 1, 2, 3, 4, 6, 9, 13, 19, 28, **41.**

Example 3: How many different ways to climb 10 stairs if one can only climb stairs two or three steps at a time?

Solution: 7.

4

This is the case 5. We need to get N_1, N_2, and N_3. $N_4 = N_2 + N_1$

We have 0 way to climb stair 1, one way to climb up to stair 2, and one way to climb up to stair 3. With the formula $N_4 = N_2 + N_1$, the sequence can be obtained as follows: 0, 1, 1, 1, 2, 2, 3, 4, 5, **7**.

Example 4: (2010 Mathcounts Handbook) A frog is going to hop up the stairs from the first floor to the second floor. Hopping up the stairs one step at a time will require a total of ten hops. If the frog can hop one, two or three steps at a time, how many different sequences of hops are possible for the frog to reach the second floor with each hop being upward?

Solution: 274.

This is the case 2. We need to get N_1, N_2, and N_3. $N_4 = N_3 + N_2 + N_1$.

We have 1 way to climb stair 1, 2 ways to climb up to stair 2 (1 +1, or 2), and 4 ways to climb up to stair 3 (1 + 1+ 1, 1 + 2, 2 + 1, 3). With the formula $N_4 = N_3 + N_2 + N_1$, the sequence can be obtained as follows: 1, 2, 4, 7, 13, 24, 44, 81, 149, **274.**

Example 5: How many ways from A to B with the shortest distance walked if you can walk one step or two steps at a time. Figure shows that there are total 5 steps from *A* to *B*.

Solution: 80.

Step 1: Count the number of routes from *A* to *B*

So we have $\binom{5}{2} = 10$ routes

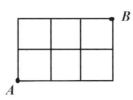

Step 2: Count the number of ways for each route.
This is the case 1. We need to get N_1 and N_2. $N_3 = N_2 + N_1$
The sequence is as follows: 1, 2, 3, 5, **8**.

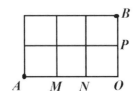

Step 3: Multiply them together to get the solution: $10 \times 8 = 80$ ways.

PROBLEMS

Problem 1: You can climb stairs with each step consisting of either 1 stair or 2 stairs. How many different ways are there to climb 10 stairs if the order of the steps is considered?

Problem 2: You have enough 1¢, 2¢, 3¢, and 4¢ stamps. You want to stick them in a row. How many ways are there to get a total of 8¢?

Problem 3: You have enough 2¢, 3¢, and 4 ¢ stamps and you want to stick them in a row. How many ways are there to get a total of 10¢?

Problem 4: How many ways from *A* to *B* with the shortest distance walked if you can walk one step or two steps at a time. Figure shows that there are total 7 steps from *A* to *B*.

SOLUTIONS:

Problem 1: Solution: 89.

This is the case 1. We need to get N_1 and N_2. $N_3 = N_2 + N_1$

The sequence is as follows: 1, 2, 3, 5, 8, 13, 21, 34, 55, **89.**

Problem 2: Solution: 108.

This is the case 3. We need to get N_1, N_2, N_3, and N_4.

Stairs	# of ways	Note
4	8	(1 + 1 + 1 + 1, 1 + 1 +2, 1 + 3, 2 + 2, 4).
3	4	(1 + 1 + 1, 1 + 2, 2 + 1, 3)
2	2	(1 + 1, or 2)
1	1	1

With the formula $N_5 = N_4 + N_3 + N_2 + N_1$, the sequence can be obtained as follows: 1, 2, 4, 8, 15, 29, 56, **108.**

Problem 3: Solution: 17.

This is the case 11. We need to get N_1, N_2, N_3, and N_4.

Stairs	# of ways	Note
4	2	(2 + 2 or 4)
3	1	(3)
2	1	(2)
1	0	

With the formula $N_5 = N_3 + N_2 + N_1$, the sequence can be obtained as follows: 0, 1, 1, 2, 2, 4, 5, 8, 11, **17**.

Problem 4: Solution: 735.

Step 1: Count the number of routes from A to B

So we have $\binom{7}{3} = 35$ routes

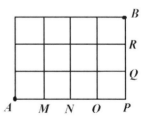

Step 2: Count the number of ways for each route.

This is the case 1. We need to get N_1 and N_2. $N_3 = N_2 + N_1$

The sequence is as follows: 1, 2, 3, 5, 8, 13, **21.**

Step 3: Multiply them together to get the solution: $35 \times 21 = 735$ ways.

Example 1: Rusty can cut a log into 3 pieces in 20 minutes. At that rate, how long will it take him to cut another such log into 6 pieces?

Solution: 50 minutes.

As shown in the figure, only 2 cuts are needed to cut the log into 3 pieces.

So it takes 10 minutes to saw through the log. To get 6 pieces you will make 5 cuts at 10 minutes each.

Note: It always takes one less cut than the number of pieces needed.

Strategy: Find time needed for one cut.

Example 2: A clock takes three seconds to strike 3 o'clock. How long does it take to strike 6 o'clock?

Solution:

It takes 1.5 seconds between each strike.

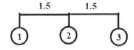

Total it takes $5 \times 1.5 = 7.5$ seconds to strike 6 o'clock.

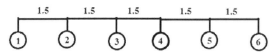

Strategy: Find time needed between strikes.

PROBLEMS

Problem 1: A log of 16 meters long is cut into 16 pieces of 1 meter long each. If it takes one minute to cut off one piece, at that rate, how long will it take to finish the job?

Problem 2: (Mathcounts) A log is cut into four pieces in 12 seconds using parallel slices. At this same rate, how many seconds will it take to cut the log into 5 pieces?

Problem 3: A log is cut into pieces of 0.5 meter long each. If it takes one minute to cut off one piece and total takes 3 minutes to do the job. What is the length of the original log?

Problem 4: A grandfather clock which strikes the number of hours every hour takes 7 seconds to strike 8 o'clock. For how many seconds each day is the clock striking?

SOLUTIONS

Problem 1: Solution:

One cut will produce two pieces. 15 cuts will do. So the total time is 15 minutes.

Problem 2: Solution:

One cut will produce two pieces. Three cut will produce four pieces. Each cut takes 12 / 3 = 4 seconds. Four cuts will produce 5 pieces. So the total time is 4 × 4 = 16 seconds.

Problem 3: Solution:

One minute will produce two pieces. Three minutes will produce 4 pieces. The length of the original log is 4 × 0.5 = 2 meters.

Problem 43: Solution:

The eight strokes at 8 o'clock are separated by seven equal intervals of time. Since the striking takes seven seconds altogether, each interval must be one second long. Similarly, at each hour the clock takes one second less than the number of the hour to strike. Thus the clock takes no time at all to strike one, it takes one second to strike two, and eleven seconds to strike twelve. The time that the clock is striking in a twelve-hour period equals the sum of the first eleven integers, and the time it is striking in a day is twice this sum. Thus the clock strikes for 132 seconds during each day.

Example 1: How many poles will you need to make a straight 15-foot fence with poles 5 feet apart?

Solution:

We divide the fence into three sections, with each section 5 feet long. We need 4 poles.

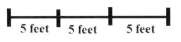

When we plant trees along a line, the loop is open.
When we plant trees around a rectangle or circle, the loop is closed.

Open Loop Formulas:

For an open loop, the number of trees planted is $N = \dfrac{L}{I} + 1$ (1)

We also have $I = \dfrac{L}{N-1}$ (2)

$$L = I(N-1) \qquad\qquad (3)$$

Where: N: number of posts

           L: total length of line or fence

           I: interval length between any 2 posts

Example 2: How many poles will you need to make a straight 96-foot fence with poles 6 feet apart?

Solution:

This is an open loop. By formula (1), the number of poles is $N = \dfrac{T}{I} + 1 = \dfrac{96}{6} + 1 = 17$.

Example 3: We have a square land with each side 20-foot long. We plan to put trees every 5 feet. How many trees do we need to have?

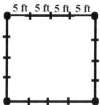

Solution:

We divide each side into four sections, with each section 5 feet long. We plant three trees each side and four trees on four corners. Total we need to plant $3 \times 4 + 4 = 16$ trees.

Closed Loop Formulas:

For a closed loop, the number of trees planted is $N = \dfrac{T}{I}$ (4)

We also have $I = \dfrac{T}{N}$ (5)

$$T = I \times N \qquad\qquad (6)$$

Example 4: (1998 Mathcounts Chapter) A gardener plans to build a fence to enclose a square garden plot. The perimeter of the plot is 96 feet, and he sets posts at the corners of the square. The posts along the sides are set 6 feet apart. How many posts will he use to fence the entire plot?

Solution: 16.

Method 1:
The loop is closed. By formula (4), the number of posts is $96/6 = 16$.

Method 2:
Since the perimeter of the square is 96, the side length is $96/4 = 24$. Each side will have 5 posts. The number of posts for the entire plot is $4 + 3 \times 4 = 16$.

PROBLEMS

Problem 1: A gardener plans to build a fence along a straight fence. He sets poles along the line 6 feet apart and he uses 17 poles. How long is the fence line?

Problem 2: Twelve identical red marbles are lined up in a row. How many blue marbles are needed if we have to put two blue marbles between any two red marbles?

Problem 3: There are 7 posts equally spaced along a circle of circumference 42 feet. What is the distance between any two posts?

Problem 4: Alex and Bob have a race to run upstairs. Alex's speed is twice f Bob's speed. It takes Bob 6 minutes to run from first floor to 4th floor. How long does it take for Alex to run from first floor to sixth floor?

Problem 5: (Mathcounts) Thirty-six fence posts were used to fence in a rectangular plot. One post was placed at each corner and the distance between adjacent posts was 5 meters. What is the number of square meters in the largest possible area for the plot?

Problem 6: (Mathcounts) If fence posts are set 10 meters apart, how many posts are needed to fence a rectangular field 400 meters by 200 meters?

SOLUTIONS

Problem 1: Solution:

This is an open loop. By formula (3), the length of the fence line is

$T = I(N-1) = 6 \times (17-1) = 96$ feet.

Problem 2: Solution:

There are $12 - 1 = 11$ spaces between twelve red marbles. So the number of blue marbles needed is $11 \times 2 = 22$.

Problem 3: Solution:

This is a closed loop. By formula (5), we have $I = \dfrac{T}{N} = \dfrac{42}{7} = 6$ feet.

Problem 4: Solution:

It takes Bob 6 minutes to walk three sections. So each section it takes Bob $6 \div 3 = 2$ minutes.

Since Alex's speed is twice of Bob's speed, it will take Alex 1 minute to walk one section.

$6 \div (4 - 1) \div 2 \times (6 - 1) = 5$.

Problem 5: Solution: 2025 (m^2).

The largest area is obtained when the plot is a square.

This is a closed loop. By formula (6), we have the perimeter $L = I \times N = 36 \times 5 = 180$.

The side length is $180/4 = 45$. The area is $45^2 = 2025$.

Problem 6: Solution: 120.

This is a closed loop. By formula (4), we have $N = \dfrac{T}{I} = \dfrac{1200}{10} = 120$ posts.

Example 1: (Mathcounts) The counting numbers are written consecutively in rows with each row containing six numbers. If the lattice continued, what is the number of the row containing 175?

Row 1:	1	2	3	4	5	6
Row 2:	7	8	9	10	11	12
Row 3:	13	14	15	16	17	18
Row 4:	18	20	21	22	23	24

Solution:

We see a pattern for every 6 integers in the table. $175 = 6 \times 29 + 1$.
So 175 is in the same column as the number 1 but in 30th row.

Example 2: (2007 Mathcounts Handbook) All the positive integers greater than 1 are arranged in five columns (_A, B, C, D, E_) as shown. Continuing the pattern, in what column will the integer 800 be written?

	A	B	C	D	E
Row 1:		2	3	4	5
Row 2:	9	8	7	6	
Row 3:		10	11	12	13
Row 4:	17	16	15	14	
Row 5:		18	19	20	21

…

Solution: B.

We see a pattern for every 8 integers in the table. 800 is the 799th number. $799 = 99 \times 8 + 7$. So 800 will be in the same column as the 7th nuber, which is 8, located in column _B_.

Example 3: (2002 State Sprint) The whole numbers are written consecutively in the pattern below. In which row (_A, B, C, D_ or _E_) will the number 500 be written?

Row A:	5	6	7		17	18	19
Row B:	4		8		16		.
Row C:	3		9		15		.
Row D:	2		10		14		.
Row E:	1		11	12	13		

Solution:

We see a pattern for every 12 integers in the table. $500 = 41 \times 12 + 8$. So 500 will be in the same column as the number 8, located in row B.

Example 4: All the positive even integers greater than 0 are arranged in five columns (*A, B, C, D,* and *E*) as shown. Continuing the pattern, in what column will the integer 50 be?

Solution: *B*.

A	B	C	D	E
	2	4	6	8
16	14	12	10	
	18	20	22	24
32	30	28	26	

Method 1: We see a pattern for every 8 integers in the table. 50 is the 25th integer and $25 = 8 \times 3 + 1$. This means that 50 is in the same column as the first number. The answer is *B*.

Method 2: Every row has 4 even integers. 50 is the $50/2 = 25^{th}$ even integer. $25 = 4 \times 6 + 1$. So 50 is the first term in the 7th row. The first term in an odd numbered row is in the column *B*, so 50 is in column *B*.

Example 5: (Mathcounts) The positive odd integers are arranged in 5 columns, *A, B, C, D,* and *E*, continuing the apttern shown. In what Column will 1599 appear?

A	B	C	D	E
	1	3	5	7
15	13	11	9	
	17	19	21	23
31	29	27	25	
	33	35	37	39

...

Solution: *A*.

We see a pattern for every 8 integers in the table. $1599 = 1 + (n - 1)2$. $n = 800$. So 1599 is the 800th number. $800 = 8 \times 9 + 8$. This means that 1959 is in the same column as the 8th number (which is 15) in the pattern. The answer is *A*.

Example 6: (Mathcounts) Suppose the numbers 1, 2, 3,... are written in a pyramid as shown. In what row does the number 100 appear?

$$1$$
$$2 \qquad 3$$
$$4 \qquad 5 \qquad 6$$
$$7 \qquad 8 \qquad 9 \qquad 10$$
$$\ldots$$

Solution:

$$1 + 2 + 3 + \ldots + n = \frac{n(n+1)}{2}.$$

We know that $\dfrac{13(13+1)}{2} = 91 < 100 < \dfrac{14(14+1)}{2} = 105$.

So 100 is in $n = 14^{\text{th}}$ row.

Example 7: (Mathcounts) When the positive integers are written in the triangular form shown, in what row does the number 1994 appear?

$$1$$
$$2 \qquad 3 \qquad 4$$
$$5 \qquad 6 \qquad 7 \qquad 8 \qquad 9$$
$$10 \qquad \ldots$$

Solution: 45.

We know that $1 + 3 + 5 + \ldots + (2n - 1) = n^2$.

Since $1936 = 44^2 < 1994 < 45^2 = 2025$, we know that the first number in the 45 row is 1937 and the last number in the 45 row is 2025.

Example 8: (2006 Mathcounts Handbook) The positive integers are written in this pattern where the number of entries in each successive row is twice the number of entries in the previous row. In which column is the number 2006?

	1	2	3	4	5	6…		
Row 1	1							
Row 2	2	3						
Row 3	4	5	6	7				
Row 4	8	9	10	11	12	13	14	15

…

Solution: 983.

We see the pattern that there are 2^i numbers in each row ($i = 0, n$).
The sum will be
$S_n = 2^0 + 2^1 + 2^2 + \ldots + 2^{n-1}$.

This is a geometric sequence and the sum is $\dfrac{2^0(1-2^n)}{1-2} = 2^n - 1$.

We see that $2^{10} = 1024 < 2006 < 2^{11} = 2048$. Thus the number 2006 is in the 11th row.

The last number is the 10th row is $2^n - 1 = 2^{10} - 1 = 1024 - 1 = 1023$.

The first number in the 11th row is 1024. 1024 is in the 1st column ($1024 - 1023 = 1$), so 2006 is in the 983 column ($2006 - 1023 = 983$).

PROBLEMS

Problem 1: The lattice shown is continued for 100 rows. What will be the third number is the 100th row?

Row 1:	1	2	3	4	5	6	7
Row 2:	8	9	10	11	12	13	14
Row 3:	15	16	17	18	19	20	21
Row 4:	22	23	24	25	26	27	28

Problem 2: All the positive even integers greater than 0 are arranged in five columns (*A, B, C, D,* and *E*) as shown. Continuing the pattern, in what column will the integer 2014 be?

A	*B*	*C*	*D*	*E*
	2	4	6	8
16	14	12	10	
	18	20	22	24
32	30	28	26	
....				

Problem 3: (AMC) The odd positive integers, 1, 3, 5, 7,…, are arranged in five columns continuing with the pattern shown on the right. Counting from the left, the column in which 1985 appears is: (A) first, (B) second, (C) third, (D) fourth, (E) fifth.

	1	3	5	7
15	13	11	9	
	17	19	21	23
31	29	27	25	
	33	35	37	39
47	45	43	41	
	49	51	53	55
.	.	.	.	
	.	.	.	.
.	.	.	.	
	.	.	.	.

Problem 4: The counting numbers are arrange in four columns as shown at the right. Under which column letter will 2014 appear?

A	B	C	D
1	2	3	4
8	7	6	5
9	10	11	12
…	14	13	

Problem 5: Suppose all the counting numbers are arranged in columns as shown at the right. Under what column-letter will 2014 appear?

A	B	C	D	E	F	G
1	2	3	4	5	6	7
8	9	10	11	12	13	14
15	16	17	18	19	_	_

Problem 6: What is the numeral that will be listed directly beneath 25 when this triangular array is continued in the same manner?

```
1
2    3
4    5    6
7    8    9    10
11   12   13   14   15
```

Problem 7: What is the number that will be listed directly beneath 25 when this triangular array is continued in the same manner?

```
              1
         2    3    4
      5    6    7    8    9
   10   11   12   13   14   15   16
```

Problem 8: In the lattice shown, 19 is the 4th number in the 3rd row. If the lattice continues in the pattern shown, what will be the 16th number in the 2nd row?

Row 4:				10			20	
Row 3:			6	9		16	19	
Row 2:		3	5	8		13	15	18
Row 1:	1	2	4	7	11	12	14	17…

20

SOLUTIONS

Problem 1: Solution: 696.
The pattern repeats every 7 numbers. The last number in the 99th row will be $99 \times 7 = 693$. The first number in the 100th row is 694. Thus the third number in that row is 696.

Problem 2: Solution: _B._
We see a pattern for every 8 integers in the table. 2014 is the 1007th integer and $1007 = 8 \times 125 + 7$. This means that 2014 is in the same column as the 7th number (14 in our case) in the first row. The answer is _B_.

Problem 3: Solution: B.
Method 1: Every row has 4 odd integers. 1985 is the 993rd odd integer. $993 = 4 \times 248 + 1$. So 1985 is the first term in 249th rows. The first number in an odd numbered row is in the column B. So 1985 is in column B.

Method 2: We see the pattern for every 8 integers in the table. 1985 is the 993rd integers and $993 = 8 \times 124 + 1$. We know that 1985 is in the same column as the first number in the first row. The answer is B.

Problem 4: Solution: C.
Method 1: We know that there are 2 even integers in every row. 2014 is the 1007th even integer. $1007 = 4 \times 251 + 3$. This means that 2014 will be in the column where the 3rd even integer located (even integer 6 in column C, in this case).

Method 2: We see the pattern in every 8 numbers. $2014 = 8 \times 251 + 6$. So 2014 is in the column where the 6th number located (integer 6 in column C, in this case).

Problem 5: Solution: E.
Method 1: We know that there are 7 even integers every two row. 2014 is the 1007th even integer. $1007 = 7 \times 143 + 6$. This means that 2014 will be in the column where the sixth even integer (12, in this case) located.

Method 2: We see the pattern in every 7 numbers. $2014 = 7 \times 287 + 5$. So 2014 is in the column where the fifth number located (column E in this case).

Problem 6: Solution: 32.

$1 + 2 + 3 + ... + n = \dfrac{n(n+1)}{2}$.

There are 7 numbers in the 7th row. 25 is in the 7th row since the last number in the 7th row is $\dfrac{7(7+1)}{2} = 28$. We count backward four times to 25: 28, 27, 26, 25.

There are 8 numbers in the 8th row. The last number in the 8th row is $\dfrac{8(8+1)}{2} = 36$. We count backward five times: 36, 35, 34, 33, 32.

So 32 is the number beneath 25.

Problem 7: Solution: 5.

Method 1:

Note that the last number in any row is a square number. So we have

10	11	12	13	14	125	16
					25	
					?	36

35 is the number directly listed below 25.

Method 2:

We know that $1 + 3 + 5 + .. + (2n - 1) = n^2$.

Since $25 = 5^2$, we know that the last number in the 5 row is 25. There are $2n - 1 = 2 \times 5 -$ 9 numbers in the 5th row.

$36 = 6^2$, we know that the last number in the 6 row is 36. There are $2n - 1 = 2 \times 6 - 1 =$ 11 numbers in the 6th row.

So there are two more numbers in 6th row. 35 is the number directly listed below 25.

Problem 8: Solution: 53.

We see a pattern for every 10 integers in the table (each section has 10 numbers). There are 3 numbers in the second row in each section. Since $16 = 3 \times 5 + 1$, The section where the 16th number in the 2nd row starts with 51 (row 1), then 52 (row 1), and 53 (row 2). So 53 is the answer.

Example 1: (1995 Mathcounts Chapter) Micah is building a corral for his pet buffalo. He equally spaces and consecutively numbers the posts as he pounds them around a circle. The seventh and seventeenth posts lie on the same diameter. How many posts are there?

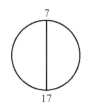

Solution: 20.
As shown in the figure, there are $(17 - 7 + 1) - 2 = 9$ numbers between 7 and 17. The number of posts is $9 \times 2 + 1 + 1 = 20$.

Example 2: The members of a girls' volleyball team have numbers from 1 through 20. They line up in numerical order and then ends of the line move around until they meet, forming a circle. What is the number of the girl across from girl number 7?

Solution:

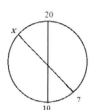

(1) Draw a circle and the diameter. Put the number 20 on the top of the circle and its half 10 on the bottom of the circle.
(2) Draw another diameter from 7 to some point x.
There are two numbers between 7 and 10 (which are 8 and 9). So there are two numbers between x and 20, which are 18 and 19. So x is number 17.

Example 3: At a party there were a total of 25 boys and girls. The girls each have a number of starting with one and going in order. The first girl dances with 6 boys, the second girl dances with the same 6 boys plus one more. This goes on until the last girl dances with all the boys. How many girls are there?

Solution:

Girls:	1	2	3	4	...	10
Boys:	6	7	8	9	...	15
Total:	7	9	11	13	...	25

There are 10 girls.

PROBLEMS

Problem 1: A group of students are standing in a circle. Each student faces someone across the circle. If student two faces student 9, how many students are in the circle?

Problem 2: At a party there were a total of 50 boys and girls. The first coming girl danced with all boys. The second girl danced with all boys but one. This went on until the last coming girl danced with 7 boys. How many boys were there?

Problem 3: (1994 Mathcounts Chapter) Twenty-six people, numbered consecutively 1 through 26, are seated equally spaced around a circular table. Which numbered person is seated directly across from person number 9?

Problem 4: At a party there were a total of 95 boys and girls. The girls each have a number of starting with one and going in order. The first girl dances with 6 boys, the second girl dances with the same 6 boys plus one more, for a total of 7 boys. The third girl dances with those 7 boys plus one more. This goes on until the last girl dances with all the boys. How many boys are there?

SOLUTIONS

Problem 1: Solution: 14.

Let the number of students be x.

(1) Draw a circle and the diameter. Put the number 20 on the top of the circle and its half 10 on the bottom of the circle.

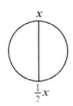

(2) Draw another diameter from 2 to some 9.

Since there is one number between x and 2 (which is "1"), so there is one number between 9 and $\frac{1}{2}x$ (which is "8"). so $\frac{1}{2}x$ should be 7. Then x is 14.

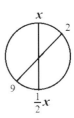

Problem 2: Solution:

Since the last girl danced with 7 boys, we know that there were more boys (7 – 1 = 6 more) than girls. Let x be the number of boys, then $x – 6$ is the number of girls. So $x + x – 6 = 50$. Solving this equation, $x = 28$.

Problem 3: Solution: 22.

(1) Draw a circle, and label 26, the last number at the top of the circle.

(2) Divide the circle into two parts, and put number 13 directly across from 26.

(3) Draw a line (the diameter) from 9 to some point x, the number of the people across from the person numbered 9. There are three points (10, 11, and 12) between 9 and 13, so there are three points between x and 26, namely 25, 24, and 23, so $x = 22$.

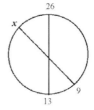

Problem 4: Solution: 50.

Number of girls:	1	2	3	4	5	…	45
Number of boys:	6	7	8	9	10	…	**50**
Total:		7	9	11	13	15	…	95.

Example 1: A rectangle kitchen floor is covered by square titles. A straight line is drawn from one corner to the corner that is diagonal opposite. How many tiles does the line cross if the floor measures exactly 8 tiles by 12 tiles?

Solution: 16.

Method 1:
We see that the diagonal of a 2 by 3 rectangle will cross 4 tiles. By proportion, a 8 by 12 rectangle will cross $4 \times 4 = 16$ tiles.

Method 2:
Using the formula $m + n - GCF (m, n)$.
$m + n = 8 + 12 = 20$. $GCF (8, 12) = 4$. We have $m + n - GCF(m, n) = 20 - 4 = 16$ tiles that the diagonal passes through.

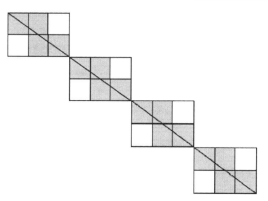

---

(1) The number of tiles crossed by the diagonal of a rectangle floor of integral dimension m by n is $N = m + n - GCF (m, n)$.

(2) The maximum number of tiles a line can cross of a rectangle floor of integral dimension m by n is $N = m + n - 1$.

(3) The maximum number of tiles a line can cross for a square floor of integral dimension n by n is $N = 2n - 1$.

Example 2: (2002 Mathcounts Chapter Sprint) A 24-foot by 72-foot rectangular dance floor is completely tiled with 1-foot by 1-foot square tiles. Two opposite corners of the dance floor are connected by a diagonal. This diagonal passes through the interior of exactly how many tiles?

Solution: 72.

The diagonal passes through $N = m + n - GCF(m, n) = 72 + 24 - 24 = 72$ tiles.

Example 3: (Mathcounts 2000 Chapter). The floor of a square room is covered with congruent square tiles. The diagonals of the room are drawn across the floor, and the two diagonals intersect a total of 9 tiles. How many tiles are on the floor?

Solution: 25.

Two diagonals intersect 9 tiles, so one diagonal intersects $(9 + 1)/2 = 5$ tiles. $m + m - m = 5$ so total tiles will be $5 \times 5 = 25$.

Example 4: A $3 \times 4 \times 5$ rectangular solid is made by gluing together $1 \times 1 \times 1$ cubes. How many of the $1 \times 1 \times 1$ cubes does an internal diagonal of this solid passes through?

Solution: 10.

The formula: $w + l + h - GCF(w, l) - GCF(l, h) - GCF(h, w) + GCF(w, l, h)$.
$w = 3; l = 4; h = 5$.
$GCF(3, 4) = 1$, $GCF(4, 5) = 1$, $GCF(3, 5) = 1$, and $GCF(3, 4, 5) = 1$.
We get the desired answer as: $3 + 4 + 5 - 1 - 1 - 1 + 1 = 10$.

For rectangular solid with width w, length l, and height h, where w, l, and h are positive integers, the number of 1 by 1 by 1 rectangular prism a diagonal passes through the interior of the rectangular solid is

$$N = w + l + h - GCF(w, l) - GCF(l, h) - GCF(h, w) + GCF(w, l, h).$$

PROBLEMS

Problem 1: (Mathcounts Competitions) A rectangular floor measuring 10 feet by 12 feet is tiled with one-foor square tiles. Throuth how many tiles would the diagonal of this rectangle pass?

Problem 2: (Mathcounts Competitions) A rectangular floor is covered with square tiles. The floor is 81 tiles long and 63 tiles wide. If a diagonal is drawn acroos the floor, how many tiles will it cross?

Problem 3: As shown in the figure, the maximum small squares a line can pass through is 3 for a 2×2 square and 5 for a 3×3 square. The maximum small squares a line can pass through for a 9×9 square is N. Find the value of N.

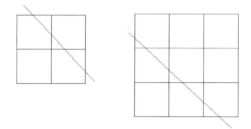

Problem 4: (2001 Mathcounts Handbook) Julian tiled a 15 feet by 21 feet rectangular ballroom with one-foot square tiles. When he finished, he drew both diagonals on the floor connecting the opposite corners of the room. What is the total number of tiles that the diagonals pass through?

Problem 5: A $15 \times 36 \times 50$ rectangular solid is made by gluing together $1 \times 1 \times 1$ cubes. An internal diagonal of this solid passes through the interiors of how many of the $1 \times 1 \times 1$ cubes?

Problem 6: (Mathcounts Competitions) Rectangle $ABCD$ has been divided into 12 unit squares as shown. Through how many squares (of any size) does segment AC pass?

SOLUTIONS

Problem 1: (Mathcounts Competitions) A rectangular floor measuring 10 feet by 12 feet is tiled with one-foor square tiles. Throuth how many tiles would the diagonal of this rectangle pass?

Solution: 20.

$m + n = 10 + 12 = 22$. $GCF(10, 12) = 2$; Using the formula, we have $m + n - GCF(m, n) = 22 - 2 = 20$ tiles that the diagonal passes through.

Problem 2: Solution: 135 (tiles).
The diagonal passes through $N = m + n - GCF(m, n) = 81 + 63 - 9 = 135$ tiles.

Problem 3: Solution: 17.
The maximum number of small squares a line can pass through for a 9×9 square $9 + 9 - 1 = 17$.

Problem 4: Solution: 63.
The number of tiles each diagonal passes through is N and
$$N = m + n - GCF(m, n) = 15 + 21 - 3 = 33.$$
Since the dimension is 15 by 21, we know that there are four 4-corners including the two end-points, so there are two 4-corners inside the given rectangle. None of the two 4-corners will be the intersection point of two diagonals. In fact, the two diagonals will meet at the center of one tile since the length of the long side of the rectangle is 21. We can easily draw a figure to show the intersection point. From the figure we know that there are three tiles common to two diagonals. Our solution is then $33 + 33 - 3 = 63$.

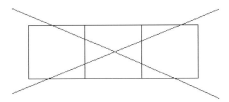

Problem 5: Solution: 92.
$w = 15 = 3 \times 5$; $l = 36 = 2^2 \times 3^2$; $h = 50 = 2 \times 5^2$.

$GCF(15, 36) = 3$, $GCF(36, 50) = 2$, $GCF(15, 50) = 5$, and $GCF(15, 36, 50) = 1$.

From formula, we get the desired answer as: $15 + 36 + 50 - 3 - 2 - 5 + 1 = 92$.

Problem 6: Solution: 14 (squares).

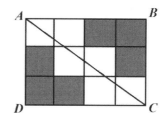

There are 6 squares that the diagonal does not touch. There are $4 \times 3 + 3 \times 2 + 2 \times 1 = 20$ squares in this figure. So the answer is $20 - 6 = 14$.

Example 1: (Mathcounts) A bug travels along the network from point A to point B. The bug can travel only south or east. Over how many different paths can the bug travel?

Solution: 10.

Method 1:

We draw the figure and count 10 paths.

Think about water flowing in pipes (line segments). The starting point is the source of the water. When two or more branches of water meet, they add and the addition carries to next segment.

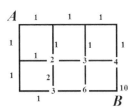

Method 2:

$$N = \frac{(m+n)!}{m! \times n!} = \frac{(2+3)!}{2! \times 3!} = \frac{5!}{2 \times 3!} = \frac{5 \times 4 \times 3!}{2 \times 3!} = 10.$$

The number of ways to walk from one corner to another corner of an m by n grid can be calculated by the following formula: $N = \binom{m+n}{n} = \binom{m+n}{m} = \frac{(m+n)!}{m! \times n!}$,

where m is the number of rows and n the number of column.

Example 2: A boy is walking along the line starting from point A to point B. Any point of intersection and line cannot be walked twice in one trip. How many ways are there?

Solution: 9.

The job (walking from A to B) is done only if he finishes two steps: walking from A to C, and walking from C to B.

The boy has 3 ways from A to C, and 3 ways from C to B. The job (walking from A to B) can be done in $3 \times 3 = 9$ ways.

Example 3: (Mathcounts) Angela wants to go from her house (located at point A) to Bernadette's house (located at point B), but she needs to stop at the market (located at point C) on the way. She may only travel to the right and down. What is the number of distinct paths that Angela can take?

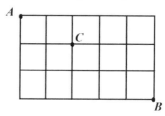

Solution: 30.

The number from ways from A to C: $N_1 = \dfrac{(1+2)!}{1! \times 2!} = 3$.

The number from ways from C to B: $N_2 = \dfrac{(2+3)!}{2! \times 3!} = 10$.

The number from ways from A to C to B: $3 \times 10 = 30$.

Example 4: (Mathcounts) The configuration shown is built from 27 segments. How many paths from A to B if one can only walks from left toward right and from down to up use these segments?

Solution: 26.

We count to 26 paths.

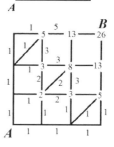

Example 5: Walking from A to B, going right or up or diagonally, how many ways are there?

Solution:

Any path must go through one of the point of $C, D, E,$ or F, it will not pass through the rest points, as shown in the figure.

A	C	B:	$2 \times 2 = 4$
A	D	B:	$4 \times 4 = 16$

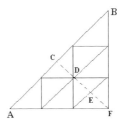

A   *E*   *B:* $1 \times 1 = 1$

A   *F*   *B:* $1 \times 1 = 1$

Total $4 + 16 + 1 + 1 = 22$ ways.

Example 6: (Mathcounts Competitions) If you must always be moving from the left toward the right, how many paths can you take from point *S* to point *T*?

Solution: 14.

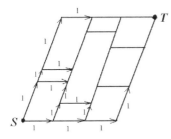
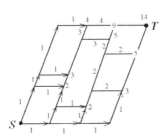

Example 7: (2005 Mathcounts National) How many continuous paths from *A* to *B*, along segments of the figure, do not revisit any of the six labeled points?

Solution: 10.

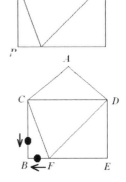

We put two dots into the figure: one is between *C* and *B* and other one is between *B* and *F*. Every path needs to go the one of the two dots. There are 4 ways going through the dot between *C* and *B* (*ACB*, *ADCB*, *ADFCB*, and *ADEFCB*).

There are 6 ways going through the dot between *F* and *B* (*ACFB*, *ACDFB*, *ACDEFB*, *ADCFB*, *ADFB*, and *ADEFB*). There are a total of **10** ways.

PROBLEMS

Problem 1: A bug travels along the network from point A to point B. The bug can travel only south or east. Over how many different paths can the bug travel?

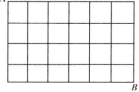

Problem 2: (Mathcounts) The only moves allowed along the edges of the figure are to the right or down. How many different paths are there from A to B?

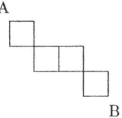

Problem 3: (Mathcounts) In the plane figure, only downward motion (movement leaving you relatively lower than where you were) is allowed. Find the total number of paths from A to B.

Problem 4: (2012 Mathcounts handbook) How many paths from A to Z can be traced following line segments on this drawing if paths must be traced in a downward direction, with no retracing?

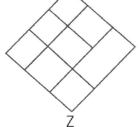

Problem 5: (Mathcounts Competitions).Using only the paths and the indicated directions, how many different routes are there from A to J?

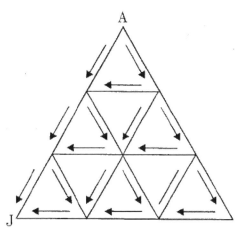

Problem 6: How many paths are there from A to E if no point or line segment can be traced twice?

SOLUTIONS

Problem 1: Solution: 210.

$$N = \frac{(6+4)!}{4!6!} = \frac{10!}{24 \times 6!} = \frac{10 \times 9 \times 8 \times 7 \times 6!}{4 \times 3 \times 2 \times 6!} = \frac{10 \times 9 \times 8 \times 7}{4 \times 3 \times 2} = 210.$$

Problem 2: Solution: 12 paths.

We have $\binom{2}{1} \times \binom{3}{1} \times \binom{2}{1} = 12$ paths.

Problem 3: Solution: 11 (paths)

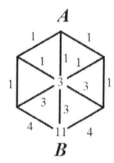

Problem 4: Solution: 17.

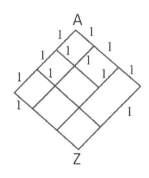

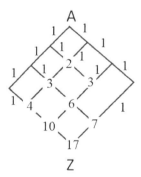

Problem 5: Solution: 22 routes.

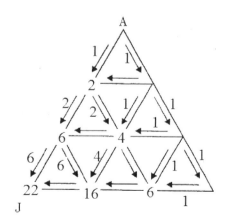

Problem 6: Solution: 14.

Every path from *A* to *E* must go through *M*, *Q*, or *N* as shown in the figure.

We count and get 14 paths.

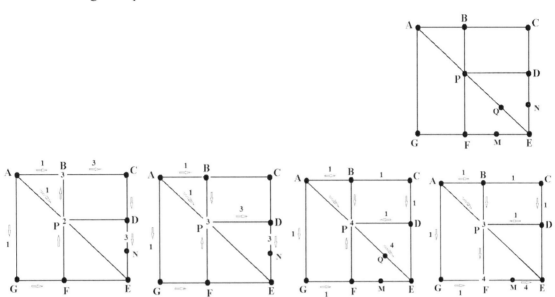

Example 1: (Mathcounts) How many distinct positive integral factors would the following product have: (12)(15)(17)?

Solution: 36.

We do prime factorization of (12)(15)(17):

$$(12)(15)(17) = 3 \times 2^2 \times 3 \times 5 \times 17 = 2^2 \times 3^2 \times 5^1 \times 17^1$$

The number of divisors $d = (2 + 1)(2 + 1)(1 + 1)(1 + 1) = 36$.

Number of divisors

For an integer n greater than 1, let the prime factorization of n be $n = p_1^a p_2^b p_3^c \ldots p_k^m$.

Where a, b, c,…, and m are nonnegative integers, p_1, p_2, …, p_k are prime numbers.

The number of divisors is: $d(n) = (a+1)(b+1)(c+1)\ldots(m+1)$.

Example 2: (Mathcounts Competitions) How many positive integer factors of 72 are even?

Solution: 9 (factors).
$72 = 3^2 \times 2^3 = 2(3^2 \times 2^2)$
Any factors of $3^2 \times 2$ will be a multiple of 2.
The number of positive even integer factors of 72 is:
$d(3^2 \times 2^2) = (2 + 1)(2 + 1) = 9$.

Number of even divisors

(1) Prime factorization of the given number.
(2) Take out one 2.
(3) Calculate the number of factors of the remaining number.

Example 3: How many odd positive integers are factors of 100?

Solution: 3.

$100 = 5^2 \times 2^2 = 2^2(5^2)$

The number of odd factors of $2^2(5^2)$ is the same as the number of factors of (5^2) which is 3.

Number of odd divisors

(1) Prime factorization of the given number.
(2) Take out all 2's.
(3) Calculate the number of factors of the remaining number.

Example 4: How many positive integer factors of 56 are also multiples of 4?

Solution: 4 (integers).

$56 = 7 \times 2^3 = 4(7 \times 2)$

The number of factors of 7×2^3 which are also multiples of 4 is the same as the number of factors of (7×2) which is 4.

Number of divisors that are the multiple of _m_

(1) Prime factorization of the given number.
(2) Take out one _m_.
(3) Calculate the number of factors of the remaining number.

PROBLEMS

Problem 1: (Mathcounts) How many positive integral factors does $2^8 \cdot 3^4 \cdot 7^6 \cdot 11$ have?

Problem 2: (Mathcounts) How many positive divisors does the number $2 \times 3^2 \times 5^3$ have?

Problem 3: What is the number of even positive integers that are divisors of 720?

Problem 4: (2004 Mathcounts Handbook) How many odd natural-number factors does $n = 2^2 \times 3^1 \times 7^2$ have?

Problem 5: (2002 Mathcounts Handbook) Handbook How many factors of 1800 are multiples of 10?

SOLUTIONS

Problem 1: Solution: 630.
The number of divisors $d = (8 + 1)(4 + 1)(6 + 1)(1 + 1) = 630$.

Problem 2: Solution: 24.
The number of divisors $d = (1 + 1)(2 + 1)(3 + 1) = 24$.

Problem 3: Solution:
Write 720 as $720 = 2^1 \times (2^3 \times 3^2 \times 5^1)$
So number of even factors can be calculated from $(2^3 \times 3^2 \times 5^1)$. That is $(3 + 1) \times (2 + 1) \times (1 + 1) = 24$

Problem 4: Solution: 6.
Write $n = 2^2 \times 3^1 \times 7^2$ as $n = 2^2 \times (3^1 \times 7^2)$.
We see that there are $2 \times 3 = 6$ factors for $3^1 \times 7^2$.
There are 6 odd factors for n.

Problem 5: Solution:
$1800 = 10 \times 180 = 10 \times (2^2 \times 3^2 \times 5)$.
The number of factors that are a multiple of 10 is the same as the number of factors of $(2^2 \times 3^2 \times 5)$, which is $(2 + 1)(2 + 1)(1 + 1) = 18$.

Example 1: (Mathcounts Handbooks) The prime factorization of a certain number is $2^2 \cdot 3^2 \cdot 5$. How many of its positive integral factors are perfect squares?

Solution: 4.
$2^2 \cdot 3^2 \cdot 5 = (2 \cdot 3)^2 \cdot 5$.
Any factors of $(2 \cdot 3)$ will be a factor of perfect square.
The answer is $(1 + 1)(1 + 1) = 4$.

Find the number of divisors that are square numbers

(1) Prime factorization of the given number.
(2) Group all integers with an even exponent and write them in the form of N^2.
(3) Take out all integers left over.
(4) Calculate the number of factors of N.

Example 2: (Mathcounts Handbooks) How many of the positive integer factors of 432 are perfect squares?

Solution: 6.

$432 = 2^4 \cdot 3^3 = (2^2 \cdot 3)^2 \cdot 3$.
Any factors of $(2^2 \cdot 3)$ will be a factor of perfect square.
The answer is $(2 + 1)(1 + 1) = 6$.

Example 3: How many perfect cube factors does $2^4 \times 3^6 \times 5^{10} \times 7^9$ have?

Solution: 96.
$2^4 \times 3^6 \times 5^{10} \times 7^9 = (2^3 \times 3^6 \times 5^9 \times 7^9) \times 2^1 \times 5^1 = (2^1 \times 3^2 \times 5^3 \times 7^3)^3 \times 2^1 \times 5^1$
$\Rightarrow \quad (2^1 \times 3^2 \times 5^3 \times 7^3)^3 \qquad \Rightarrow \quad N = 2^1 \times 3^2 \times 5^3 \times 7^3$
$d(N) = (1 + 1)(2 + 1)(3 + 1)(3 + 1) = 2 \times 3 \times 4 \times 4 = 96$.

Find the number of divisors that are cubic numbers

(1) Prime factorization of the given number.
(2) Group all integers with an odd exponent that is a multiple of 3 and write them in the form of N^3.
(3) Take out all integers left over.
(4) Calculate the number of factors of N.

Example 4: (2007 Mathcounts Handbooks) How many positive perfect cube factors does $2^4 \times 3^6 \times 5^{10} \times 7^9$ have?

Solution: 96.

$2^4 \times 3^6 \times 5^{10} \times 7^9 = 2 \times 5 \times (2^3 \times 3^6 \times 5^9 \times 7^9) = 2 \times 5 \times (2^1 \times 3^2 \times 5^3 \times 7^3)^3$.
There are$(1 + 1)(2 + 1)(3 + 1)(3 + 1) = 2 \times 3 \times 4^2 = 96$ perfect cube factors.

PROBLEMS

Problem 1: How many perfect squares are divisors of $2^3 \times 3^4$?

Problem 2: How many cubic are divisors of $2^3 \times 3^4$?

Problem 3: (2004 Mathcounts Handbook) How many odd perfect square factors does $2^4 \times 3^6 \times 5^{10} \times 7^9$ have?

Problem4: (AMC) How many perfect cube factors does $2^4 \times 3^6 \times 5^{10}$ have?

Problem 5: (AMC) How many perfect squares are divisors of the product $1! \times 2! \times 3! \times 4! \times 5! \times 6! \times 7! \times 8! \times 9$?

SOLUTIONS

Problem 1: Solution:

$$2^3 \times 3^4 = 2\,(2^2 \times 3^4) = 2(2^1 \times 3^2)^2$$

The number of perfect square divisors = $(1 + 1)(2 + 1) = 6$

Problem 2: Solution:

$$2^3 \times 3^4 = 3 \times (2^3 \times 3^3) = 3 \times (2^1 \times 3^1)^3$$
The number of cubic divisors = $(1 + 1)(1 + 1) = 4$.

Problem 3: Solution : 120.
$$2^4 \times 3^6 \times 5^{10} \times 7^9 = 7 \times 2^4\,(3^6 \times 5^{10} \times 7^8) = 7 \times 2^4\,(3^3 \times 5^5 \times 7^4)^2 \;.$$
There are $(3 + 1)\,(5 + 1)\,(4 + 1) = 4 \times 6 \times 5 = 120$ odd perfect square factors.

Problem4: (AMC) How many perfect cube factors does $2^4 \times 3^6 \times 5^{10}$ have?

Solution: 24.

$$2^4 \times 3^6 \times 5^{10} = 2(\,2 \times 5 \times (2^3 \times 3^6 \times 5^9) = 2 \times 5 \times (2^1 \times 3^2 \times 5^3)^3$$
There are $(1 + 1)\,(2 + 1)(3 + 1) = 2 \times 3 \times 4 = 24$ perfect cube factors.

Problem 5: Solution: 672.

$$1 \times 2 \times (3 \times 2) \times (4 \times 3 \times 2) \times (5 \times 4 \times 3 \times 2) \times (6 \times 5 \times 4 \times 3 \times 2) \times (7 \times 6 \times 5 \times 4 \times 3 \times 2) \times (8 \times 7 \times 6 \times 5 \times 4 \times 3 \times 2) \times (9 \times 8 \times 7 \times 6 \times 5 \times 4 \times 3 \times 2)$$
$$= 2^{30} \times 3^{13} \times 5^5 \times 7^3 = (2^{30} \times 3^{12} \times 5^4 \times 7^2) \times 3^1 \times 5^1 \times 7^1$$
$$= (2^{15} \times 3^6 \times 5^2 \times 7^1)^2 \times 3^1 \times 5^1 \times 7^1.$$
The number of perfect square divisors = $(15 + 1)(6 + 1)(2 + 1)(1 + 1) = 672$.

Example 1: (Mathcounts) Six softball teams are to play each other once. How many games are needed?

Solution: 15.

Method 1:
Team A plays five games. Team B plays four new games, and so on. The total number of games is $5 + 4 + 3 + 2 + 1 = 15$.

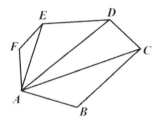   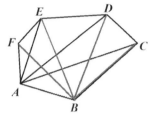

Method 2:

Since each game involves two teams, the total number of games will be $\binom{6}{2} = 15$.

Example 2: (Mathcounts) If each of ten people at a meeting shake hands with each other, how many handshakes will there be?

Solution: 45 handshakes.

Since there are two people involved with each handshake, the total number of handshakes the 10 people will make is $\binom{10}{2} = 45$.

Example 3: (Mathcounts) Eight volleyball teams are to play each other twice. How many games are needed?

Solution: 56 games.

$2 \times \binom{8}{2} = 2 \times 28 = 56$.

Handshakes. There are n people in a party. Each two people shake hands once. The number of handshakes is $\binom{n}{2} = \dfrac{n(n-1)}{2}$.

Tournament. n baseball teams have a tournament. Every two teams compete only once. The number of games is $\binom{n}{2} = \dfrac{n(n-1)}{2}$.

Tournament. n baseball teams have a tournament. Every two teams compete two times.

The number of games is $2\binom{n}{2} = n(n-1)$.

Example 4: (2008 Mathcounts Chapter) Five couples were at a party. If each person shook hands exactly once with everyone else except his/her spouse, how many handshakes were exchanged? (Note: One obviously doesn't shake hands with oneself.)

Solution: 40.

The total possible number of handshakes the 5 couples (10 people) will make is $\dfrac{n(n-1)}{2} = \dfrac{10 \times 9}{2} = 45$.

Since nobody shook hands with his/her spouse, the answer is then $45 - 5 = 40$.

Example 5: At a party each man shook hands with everyone except his wife. There were no handshakes between women. Six married couples attended the party. How many handshakes were there between 12 people?

Solution: 45.

The total possible number of handshakes the 6 couples (12 people) will make is $\dfrac{n(n-1)}{2} = \dfrac{12 \times 11}{2} = 66$.

Since nobody shook hands with his/her spouse, the answer is then $66 - 6 = 60$.

Since there were no handshakes between women, and the possible number of handshakes between women is $\dfrac{6(6-1)}{2} = \dfrac{6 \times 5}{2} = 15$, the answer is then $60 - 15 = 45$.

Example 6: (2012 AMC 8) In the BIG N, a middle school football conference, each team plays every other team exactly once. If a total of 21 conference games were played during the 2012 season, how many teams were members of the BIG N conference?

(A) 6   (B) 7   (C) 8   (D) 9   (E) 10

Solution: 7.

Since there are two teams involved with each game, the total number of games n teams will play is $\dbinom{n}{2} = \dfrac{n(n-1)}{2}$.

Then we have $\dfrac{n(n-1)}{2} = 21 \implies (n-1)n = 2 \times 21 = 6 \times 7$.

So $n = 7$.

Example 7: At a party, every two people shook hands once. How many people attended the party if there were 66 handshakes?

Solution: 40.

Since there are two people involved with each handshake, the total number of handshakes the n people will make is $\dbinom{n}{2} = \dfrac{n(n-1)}{2}$.

Then we have $\dfrac{n(n-1)}{2} = 66 \implies (n-1)n = 2 \times 66 = 11 \times 12$.

So $n = 12$.

Example 8: In the BIG N, a middle school football conference, each team plays every other team exactly twice. If a total of 132 conference games were played during the 2015 season, how many teams were members of the BIG N conference?

Solution: 12.

Since there are two teams involved with each game, the total number of games n teams

will play is $2\binom{n}{2} = 2 \times \dfrac{n(n-1)}{2} = (n-1)n$.

Then we have $(n-1)n = 132 = 11 \times 12$.

So $n = 12$.

PROBLEMS

Problem 1: (Mathcounts Competitions) There are eight schools in an athletic conference. How many games must be scheduled for each school's team to play every other conference team one time?

Problem 2: (Mathcounts) Thirteen people attend a party. During the party everyone shakes hands with everyone else. How many handshakes take place at the party?

Problem 3: (Mathcounts) There are ten teams in a school district competition. Each team plays each other team twice. What is the total number of games played in the competition?

Problem 4: (Mathcounts) A softball league has 8 teams. During the season, each team plays each of the other teams exactly 3 times. What is the total number of games played by all teams?

Problem 5: (Mathcounts) At a women's double tennis tournament, there were three teams of two women. After the tournament, each woman shook hands once with each of the other players except her partner. What is the number of handshakes that occurred?

Problem 6: (Mathcounts) In a single tennis tournament, each player plays every other player exactly once. There is a total of 28 games. How many players are in the tournament?

Problem 7: On a meeting every guest shakes hands, exactly once, with every other guest. There are 36 handshakes between women and 28 handshakes between men. Find the number of handshakes between women and men.

Problem 8: (Mathcounts) Sixteen people attended a party, and each person brought a gift for everyone else at the party. Altogether how many gifts were brought to the party?

Problem 9: (1990 AMC) At one of George Washington's parties, each man shook hands with everyone except his spouse, and no handshakes took place between women. If 13 married couples attended, how many handshakes were there among these 26 people?
    (A) 78   (B) 185   (C) 234   (D) 321   (E) 325

SOLUTIONS

Problem 1: Solution: 28.

Since each game involves two teams, the total number of games will be $\binom{8}{2} = 28$.

Problem 2: Solution: 78.

Since each handshake involves two people, the total number of handshakes will be $\binom{13}{2} = 78$.

Problem 3: Solution: 90.

Since each game involves two teams and since each team plays each other team twice,

the total number of games will be $2\binom{n}{2} = 2\binom{10}{2} = 2 \times 45 = 90$.

Problem 4: Solution: 84.

Since each game involves two teams and since each team plays each other team 3 times,

the total number of games will be $3\binom{n}{2} = 3\binom{8}{2} = 3 \times 28 = 84$.

Problem 5: Solution: 12.

Since each handshake involves two people, the total possible number of handshakes will

be $\binom{6}{2} = 15$.

Since each woman did not shake hands with her partner, the answer is $15 - 3 = 12$.

Problem 6: Solution: 8 players.

Since each game accounts for two players, the total number of games the n players will

play $\binom{n}{2} = \dfrac{n(n-1)}{2}$.

Then we have $\dfrac{n(n-1)}{2} = 28 \quad \Rightarrow \quad (n-1)n = 2 \times 28 = 7 \times 8$.

So $n = 8$.

Problem 7: Solution: 72.

The number of handshakes between women is $\binom{n}{2} = \dfrac{n(n-1)}{2}$.

Then we have $\dfrac{n(n-1)}{2} = 36 \implies (n-1)n = 2 \times 36 = 8 \times 9$.

So $n = 9$. The number of women is 9.

Similarly we get the number of men is 8.

The number of handshakes between women and men is $9 \times 8 = 72$.

Problem 8: Solution: 240 gifts.

Each person brought 16 - 1 = 15 gifts.

The answer is $16 \times 15 = 240$.

Problem 9: Solution: 234.

If Alex shakes hand with Bob or Bob shakes hand with Alex, their interaction only counts as one time, so the order does not matter and we may use combinations to solve this problem.

We have 26 people, so at most we can have $\binom{26}{2}$ handshakes. Among these handshakes,

there are $\binom{13}{2}$ handshakes between women, and 13 handshakes between spouses.

Therefore the final answer is $\binom{26}{2} - \binom{13}{2} - 13 = 234$.

Example 1: (Mathcounts) How many distinct diagonals does a regular hexagon have?

Solution: 9.

Method 1:
We draw all the diagonals. From each of the vertices A and B, we are able to draw three diagonals. From the vertex C, we are able to draw two new diagonals. From the vertex D, we are able to draw one new diagonal. From the vertices E and F, we are not able to draw any new diagonal. The total is $3 + 3 + 2 + 1 = 9$.

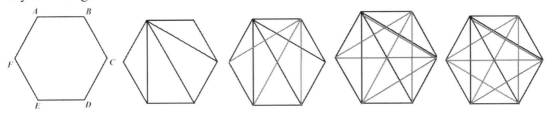

Method 2:

Any two points will form a line. So we have $\binom{6}{2}$ lines. Of them, the line formed by two adjacent points (which is a side of the hexagon) is not a diagonal. So we have

$\binom{6}{2} - 6 = 15 - 6 = 9$ diagonals.

Number of Diagonals

The number of diagonals of a convex n-gon is N and $N = \binom{n}{2} - n = \dfrac{n(n-3)}{2}$.

Name	Sides	Name	Sides
Quadrilateral	4	Pentagon	5
Hexagon	6	Heptagon	7
Octagon	8	Decagon	10
Dodecagon	12		

Example 2: (Mathcounts Handbooks) Find the number of degrees in the measure of each interior angle of a regular pentagon.

Solution: 108°.

$$a = 180 - \frac{360}{n} = 180 - \frac{360}{5} = 108.$$

> Sum of interior angles of convex n – gon = $(n - 2) \times 180°$.
>
> The formula to determine the degree measure a of each interior angle of a regular n-sided polygon: $a = 180 - \frac{360}{n}$

Example 3: (Mathcounts Competitions) A regular polygon has 27 diagonals. What is the number of degrees in the measure of an interior angle of the polygon?

Solution: 140 (degrees).

$$\frac{n(n-3)}{2} = 27 \qquad \Rightarrow \qquad (n-3)n = 2 \times 27 = 2 \times 3 \times 3 \times 3 = 6 \times 9.$$

So $n = 9$ and $a = 180 - \frac{360}{n} = 180 - \frac{360}{9} = 140$.

Example 4: (Mathcounts) How many diagonals does a regular heptagon have?

Solution: 14.

A regular heptagon has 7 sides. The number of diagonals is $N = \frac{n(n-3)}{2} = \frac{7(7-3)}{2} = 14$.

Example 5: (Mathcounts Handbooks) A polygon has n sides has n diagonals. What is n?

Solution: 5.

$$n = \frac{n(n-3)}{2} \quad \Rightarrow \quad 2n = n(n-3) \quad \Rightarrow \quad n^2 - 5n = 0 \quad \Rightarrow \quad n = 5.$$

Example 6: (Mathcounts Competitions) Each interior angle of a regular polygon measures $140°$. How many sides does the polygon have?

Solution: 9 (sides).

$$a = 180 - \frac{360}{n} \quad \Rightarrow \quad 140 = 180 - \frac{360}{n} \quad \Rightarrow \quad \frac{360}{n} = 40 \quad \Rightarrow \quad n = \frac{360}{40} = 9.$$

Example 7: An interior angle of a regular polygon is five times the size of an exterior angle. How many sides does the polygon have?

Solution: 12.

The exterior angle and the interior angle are supplementary.
Let the interior angle be $5x$.
$5x + x = 180° \qquad \Rightarrow \qquad 5x = 150°$
We know that $a = 180 - \frac{360}{n}$.

$$150 = 180 - \frac{360}{n} \quad \Rightarrow \quad \frac{360}{n} = 30 \quad \Rightarrow \quad n = \frac{360}{30} = 12.$$

Example 8: (Mathcounts Handbooks) How many diagonals does an octagon have?

Solution: 20 (diagonals)

An octagon has 8 sides. The number of diagonals is $N = \frac{n(n-3)}{2} = \frac{8(8-3)}{2} = 20$.

PROBLEMS

Problem 1: (Mathcounts Handbooks) The number of degrees in the measures of the interior angles of a convex pentagon are five consecutive integers. Determine the number of degrees in the largest angle

Problem 2: (Mathcounts Handbooks) A convex polygon with n sides has 14 diagonals. How many diagonals does an $(n + 1)$-sided convex polygon have?

Problem 3: Given that a convex polygon with n sides has $10n$ diagonals, what is the value of n?   (Mathcounts Handbooks)

Problem 4: (Mathcounts Handbooks) What is the number of sides of a convex polygon that has 35 distinct diagonals?

Problem 5: (Mathcounts Handbooks) If exactly five diagonals can be drawn from one vertex of a convex polygon, how many sides does the polygon have?

Problem 6: (Mathcounts Competitions) The exterior angles of a regular polygon each measure 20°. How many sides does the polygon have?

Problem 7: (Mathcounts Handbooks) A regular polygon has interior angles of 120 degrees. How many sides does the polygon have?

Problem 8: (Mathcounts Competitions) If a convex polygon has 90 distinct diagonals, how many sides does it have?

SOLUTIONS:

Problem 1: Solution: 110.

Sum of interior angles of pentagon $= (n - 2) \times 180° = (5 - 2) \times 180° = 540$.

Let the largest angle be x.

$x + (x - 1) + (x - 2) + (x - 3) + (x - 4) = 540 \Rightarrow 5x - 10 = 540 \Rightarrow x = 110$.

Problem 2: Solution: 20.

The number of diagonals is $\dfrac{n(n-3)}{2} = 14 \Rightarrow (n-3)n = 2 \times 14 = 4 \times 7 \Rightarrow n = 7$.

The number of diagonals an $(7 + 1)$-sided convex polygon is $\dfrac{n(n-3)}{2} = \dfrac{8(8-3)}{2} = 20$.

Problem 3: Solution: 23.

$\dfrac{n(n-3)}{2} = 10n \Rightarrow (n-3)n = 20n \Rightarrow n^2 - 23n = 0 \Rightarrow \qquad n = 23$.

Problem 4: Solution: 10.

$\dfrac{n(n-3)}{2} = 35 \Rightarrow \qquad (n-3)n = 2 \times 35 = 7 \times 10$. So $n = 10$.

Problem 5: Solution: 8.

We draw the figure and we get 8 sides.

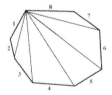

Problem 6: Solution: 18 (sides).

The exterior angle and the interior angle are supplementary.

The interior angle is $180° - 20° = 160°$.

We know that $a = 180 - \dfrac{360}{n}$. $160 = 180 - \dfrac{360}{n} \Rightarrow \dfrac{360}{n} = 20 \Rightarrow n = \dfrac{360}{20} = 18$.

Problem 7: Solution: 6.

$120 = 180 - \dfrac{360}{n} \Rightarrow \dfrac{360}{n} = 60 \Rightarrow n = \dfrac{360}{60} = 6$.

Problem 8: Solution: 15 (sides)

$\dfrac{n(n-3)}{2} = 90 \Rightarrow \qquad (n-3)n = 2 \times 90 = 12 \times 15$. So $n = 15$.

The following terms have the same meanings: last digit, ones digit, and units digit.

Patterns of the last digit of a^n

The last digits of a^n have patterns shown in the table below.

For example, when $a = 2$,

$$2^1 = 2 \qquad 2^2 = 4, \qquad 2^3 = 8, \qquad 2^4 = 16,$$
$$2^5 = 32, \qquad 2^6 = 64, \qquad 2^7 = 128, \qquad 2^8 = 256,\ldots$$

The last digits of 2^n demonstrate a pattern: 2, 4, 8, 6, 2, 4, 8, 6, etc…

Similarly we have

n	1	2	3	4	Period
1^n	1				1
2^n	2	4	8	6	4
3^n	3	9	7	1	4
4^n	4	6			2
5^n	5				1
6^n	6				1
7^n	7	9	3	1	4
8^n	8	4	2	6	4
9^n	9	1			2

Theorem: The last digit of a^{4k+r} is the same as the last digit of a^r, where $r = 1, 2, 3,$ or 4 and k is a positive integer.

Example 1: (Mathcounts Handbooks) What is the units digit in the number named by 2^{48}?

Solution: 6.

The pattern for the last digit of 2^n is 2, 4, 8, 6, etc.
$48 \div 4 = 12$.

In other words, the last digit of 2^{48} is the same as the last digit of 2^4.
So the last digit is 6.

Example 2: (Mathcounts handbooks Find the units digit of 7^{22}

Solution: 9.

The pattern for the last digit is: 7, 9, 3, 1, 7, 9, 3, 1, etc.
When 22 is divided by 4, the quotient is 5 and the remainder is 2. The last digit of 7^{22} is the same as the last digit of 7^2, so the last digit is 9.

Example 3: Find the last digit of 3^{1999}.

Solution: 7.

The pattern for the last digits of 3^n is: 3, 9, 7, 1 (repeating every four numbers).
When 1999 is divided by 4, the quotient is 499 and the remainder is 3. The last digit of 3^{1999} is the same as the last digit of 3^3. So the last digit of 3^{1999} is 7.

Example 4: What is the units digit of 1998^{1998}? (Mathcounts competitions)

Solution: 4.

The units digit of 1998^{1998} is the same as the units digit of 8^{1998}.
The pattern for the last digit is: 8, 4, 2, 6, 8, 4, 2, 6, etc.
When 1998 is divided by 4, the quotient is 499 and the remainder is 2. The last digit of 8^{1998} is the same as the last digit of 8^2, so the last digit is 4.

PROBLEMS

Problem 1: (Mathcounts) What is the units digit in the number named by 4^{81}?

Problem 2: (Mathcounts Handbooks) What will be the units digit of 2^{26}?

Problem 3: (Mathcounts Handbooks) In what digit does 3^{571} end?

Problem 4: What is the units digit of 1997^{1997}? (Mathcounts competitions)

Problem 5: Find the units digit of $3^{1986} - 2^{1986}$. (Mathcounts competitions)

SOLUTIONS

Problem 1: Solution: 4.

The pattern for the last digit of 4^n is 4, 6, 4, 6, etc.

When 81 is divided by 4, the quotient is 20 and the remainder is 1. Therefore, the last digit of 4^{81} is the same as the last digit of 4^1. So the last digit is 4.

Problem 2: Solution: 4.

The pattern for the last digit of 2^n is 2, 4, 8, 6, etc.

When 81 is divided by 4, the quotient is 20 and the remainder is 1. Therefore, the last digit of 4^{81} is the same as the last digit of 4^1. So the last digit is 4.

Problem 3: Solution: 7.

The pattern for the last digits of 3^n is: 3, 9, 7, 1 (repeating every four numbers).

When 571 is divided by 4, the quotient is 142 and the remainder is 3. The last digit of 3^{571} is the same as the last digit of 3^3. So the last digit of 3^{571} is 7.

Problem 4: Solution: 7.

The last digit of 1997^{1997} is the same as the last digit of 7^{1997}.

$7^{1997} = 7^{499 \times 4 + 1}$ is the same as the last digit of 7^1. So the last digit of 1997^{1997} is 7.

Problem 5: Solution: 5.

The last digit of $3^{1986} = 3^{496 \times 4 + 2}$ is the same as the last digit of 3^2. So the last digit of 3^{1986} is 9.

The last digit of $2^{1986} = 2^{496 \times 4 + 2}$ is the same as the last digit of 2^2. So the last digit of 2^{1986} is 5. $9 - 4 = 5$. So the answer is 5.

Example 1: (1995 Mathcounts State Competition Sprint) In this rectangular array, the dots are one inch apart horizontally and vertically. What is the number of square inches in the area of the polygon shown? Express your answer as a mixed number.

Solution: $6\dfrac{1}{2}$.

We count that the number of points is 5 inside the figure and 5 on the boundary.

By the Pick's Theorem, the area is $A = \dfrac{B}{2} + I - 1 = \dfrac{5}{2} + 5 - 1 = 6\dfrac{1}{2}$.

Find the area of the region bounded by grids (Pick's law)

For unit rectangular grid: $Area = \dfrac{B}{2} + I - 1$.

For unit triangular grid: $Area = B + 2I - 2$

B: Number of boundary points. I: Number of interior point.

Example 2: Find the area of pentagon *ABCDE* in the following unit triangular grid.

Solution: 31.

We count that the number of points is 14 inside the figure and 5 on the boundary.

By the Pick's Theorem, the area is $B + 2I - 2 = 2 \times 14 + 5 - 2 = 31$.

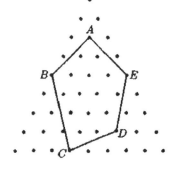

Example 3: A polygon of area 6 is drawn with its vertices on the points of a lattice. There are six lattice points on the boundary of the polygon. How many points are in the polygon's interior?

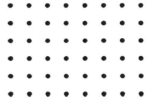

Solution: 4.

Pick's theorem states that the area of a polygon whose vertices are lattice points can be found by using the following formula $A = \dfrac{B}{2} + I - 1$.

Thus $\dfrac{6}{2} + I - 1 = 6 \quad \Rightarrow \quad I = 7 - 3 = 4$.

Example 4: A polygon of area 10 is drawn with its vertices on the points of a lattice. There are four lattice points in the polygon's interior. How many lattice points on the boundary of the polygon.?

Solution: 9.

Pick's theorem states that the area of a polygon whose vertices are lattice points can be found by using the following formula $A = \dfrac{B}{2} + I - 1$.

Thus $\dfrac{6}{2} + I - 1 = 10 \quad \Rightarrow \quad I = 11 - 3 = 9$.

PROBLEMS

Problem 1: Find the area of each polygon.

a. 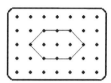   *b.*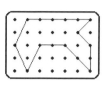

Problem 2: In this square array, the dots are one inch apart horizontally and vertically. What is the number of square inches in the area of the polygon shown? Express your answer as a mixed number.

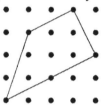

Problem 3: (2003 Mathcounts Handbook) The horizontally and vertically adjacent points in this square grid are 1 cm apart. How many square centimeters are in the area of square $ABCD$?

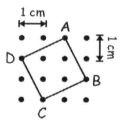

Problem 4: A polygon of area 6 square units is drawn with its vertices on the points of a lattice. There are m lattice points on the boundary of the polygon and n points in the polygon's interior. m and n are positive integers. How many possible values of n are there?

Problem 5: Find the area of triangle ABC in the following unit triangular grid.

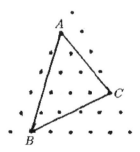

SOLUTIONS

Problem 1: Solution a: $A = 8/2 + 3 - 1 = 6$
Solution b: $A = 16/2 + 7 - 1 = 14$

Problem 2: Solution: $7\frac{1}{2}$.

We count that the number of points is 6 inside the figure and 5 on the boundary.

By the Pick's Theorem, the area is $A = \dfrac{B}{2} + I - 1 = \dfrac{5}{2} + 6 - 1 = 7\dfrac{1}{2}$.

Problem 3: Solution: 5.
Pick's theorem states that the area of a polygon whose vertices are lattice points can be

found by using the following formula $A = \dfrac{B}{2} + I - 1 = \dfrac{4}{2} + 4 - 1 = 5$.

Problem 4: Solution: 6.
Pick's theorem states that the area of a polygon whose vertices are lattice points can be

found by using the following formula $\dfrac{B}{2} + I - 1 = 6 \implies B + 2I = 14$.

When $I = 0$, $B = 14$.   When $I = 1$, $B = 12$.   When $I = 2$, $B = 10$.
When $I = 3$, $B = 8$.   When $I = 4$, $B = 6$.   When $I = 5$, $B = 4$.
When $I = 6$, $B = 2$ which is not possible since any polygon needs to have at least three sides.
There are 6 possible values for B. The answer is 6.

Problem 5: Solution: 17.
Method 1:
By the Pick's law, we have $B = 3$ and $I = 8$.
$Area = B + 2I - 2 = 3 + 2 \times 8 - 2 = 17$.
Method 2:
Connect E, C, and F and then connect DC, EA, and FB.
Parallelogram $ADCD'$: Area $\triangle ADC = 3$;
Parallelogram $AEBE'$: Area $\triangle ABE = 4$;
Parallelogram $BF'CF$: Area $\triangle BCF = 6$;
Area $\triangle DEF = 4$; Area $\triangle ABC = \triangle ADC + \triangle ABE + \triangle BCF + \triangle DEF = 3 + 4 + 6 + 4 = 17$.

Example 1: A rectangle is divided into four smaller rectangles A, B, C, and D as shown in the figure. If the areas of rectangles A, B, and C are 27 cm^2, 36 cm^2, and 45 cm^2, respectively, and if each of these rectangles has integral dimensions, what is the area in square centimeters of rectangle D?

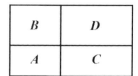

B	D
A	C

Solution: 60 (cm^2).

$$a \times b = c \times d \qquad \Rightarrow \qquad 27 \times D = 36 \times 45 \qquad \Rightarrow \qquad D = 60.$$

Example 2: Each rectangular region in the figure has the area shown: the largest region has area 48 in^2; another region has area 12 in^2; and the other two regions have the same unknown area x in^2. All dimensions are whole numbers. What is the number of inches in the difference between the greatest and least possible perimeters for the entire rectangle?

x	48
12	x

Solution: 36.

b		
a 12	12	12
12	12	12
12	12	12

$$x \times x = 12 \times 48 \qquad \Rightarrow \qquad x^2 = 12 \times 48 \quad \Rightarrow \quad x = 24.$$

The given rectangle can be divided as follows:

Let the sides of the small rectangle be a and b. $a \times b = 12$.

The greatest possible perimeter of the entire rectangle is obtained by letting a and b as far as possible. So $a = 1$ and $b = 12$.

The least possible perimeter of the entire rectangle is obtained by letting a and b be as close as possible. So $a = 3$ and $b = 3$.

The perimeter will be $2(3a + 3b) = 6(a + b)$.

The difference will be $6(1 + 12) - 6(3 + 4) = 36$.

Let a, b, c, and d represent the area of each corresponding rectangle. Then $a \times b = c \times d$.

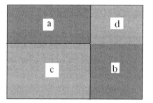

Example 3: As shown in the figure, P is a point inside rectangle $ABCD$. $\triangle ABP$, $\triangle BCP$, and $\triangle CDP$ have the areas of 24 cm^2, 20 cm^2, and 48 cm^2, respectively. What is the area of $\triangle DAP$ in square centimeters?

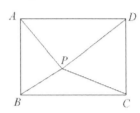

Solution: 52.

$$S_{\triangle ABP} + S_{\triangle CDP} = S_{\triangle BCP} + S_{\triangle DAP} .$$

$$\Rightarrow \quad 24 + 48 = 20 + S_{\triangle DAP} \quad \Rightarrow \quad S_{\triangle DAP} = 52 \ cm^2$$

> Parallelogram $ABCD$, P is any interior point, we have always:
>
> $$S_{\triangle PAB} + S_{\triangle PCD} = \frac{1}{2} \times S_{ABCD} .$$

Example 4: (2005 Mathcounts National Target) A point inside a square is positioned so that the distances to the four vertices are 27, 21, 6 and x units. If x is a whole number, what is the value of x?

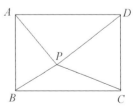

Solution: 18.

Let a, b, c, and d represent the distances to the four vertices.
Then $a^2 + b^2 = c^2 + d^2$
Substituting in the values, $27^2 + 6^2 = 21^2 + d^2 \quad \Rightarrow \quad d = 18$.

> For any point P on the plane of rectangle $ABCD$, we have always:
> $$AP^2 + PC^2 = BP^2 + PD^2$$

PROBLEMS

Problem 1: (Mathcounts) The figure shown is composed of rectangles A, B, C, And D with whole number values for length and width. The areas of regions A, B, D, in square meters, are shown in the diagram. What is the area in square meters of rectangle C?

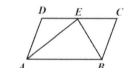

Problem 2: (Mathcounts) A rectangular garden is separated into four smaller rectangles. The area of rectangle B is 60 square meters, the area of square C is 16 square meters, and the area of rectangle D is 48 square meters. What is the number of meters in the perimeter of the garden?

Problem 3: (Mathcounts) What is the ratio of the area of $\triangle AEB$ to the area of the parallelogram $ABCD?$

Problem 4: (Mathcounts) If $ACDE$ is a square whose edge measures 12 cm, what is the area of the shaded region?

Problem 5: $STMP$ is a rectangle. $SP = 10$ and $PM = 18$. Find the number of square units in the area of $\triangle PWM$.

Problem 6: A point inside a square is positioned so that the distances to the four vertices are 23, 11, 17 and x units. If x is a whole number, what is the value of $x?$

SOLUTIONS

Problem 1: Solution: 48 m^2.

$A \times D = B \times C \qquad \Rightarrow \qquad 40 \times 30 = 25 \times C \qquad \Rightarrow \qquad C = 48$.

Problem 2: Solution: 50.

$A \times D = B \times C \Rightarrow \qquad A \times 48 = 60 \times 16 \qquad \Rightarrow \qquad x^2 = 12 \times 48 \quad \Rightarrow \qquad A = 20$.

The given rectangle can be divided as follows:

The perimeter will be $2(9 + 16) = 50$.

5	20	20	20	20
4	16	16	16	16

4

Problem 3: Solution: 1:2.

$S_{\Delta EAD} + S_{\Delta EBC} = \dfrac{1}{2} \times S_{ABCD} \qquad \Rightarrow \qquad \dfrac{S_{\Delta EAD} + S_{\Delta EBC}}{S_{ABCD}} = \dfrac{1}{2}$.

Problem 4: Solution: 72 cm^2.

$S_{\Delta AEB} + S_{\Delta CDB} = \dfrac{1}{2} \times S_{ABCD} \qquad \Rightarrow S_{\Delta AEB} + S_{\Delta CDB} = \dfrac{1}{2} \times 12^2 = 72$.

Problem 5: Solution: 90.

$S_{\Delta SPW} + S_{\Delta TMW} = \dfrac{1}{2} \times S_{ABCD} = S_{\Delta PWM} = \dfrac{1}{2} \times 10 \times 18 = 90$.

Problem 6: Solution: 19.

Let a, b, c, and d represent the distances to the four vertices. Then $a^2 + b^2 = c^2 + d^2$

Substituting in the values, $23^2 + 11^2 = 17^2 + d^2 \; \Rightarrow \; d = 19$.

Example 1: Which vertices meet with vertex 1 when the net below is folded?

Solution: Vertices 1, 2 and 3.

Step 1. Draw a line across **_TWO_** square faces, that is, draw a line from the given vertex 1 to point O.

Step 2. Find other points that are the same distance to point O. In this case find the points 2 and 3. Draw lines from points 2 and 3 to point O.

Step 3. Conclusion: Vertices 1, 2 and 3 will meet when the net is folded.

**Note that for a cube, three faces share one vertex.**

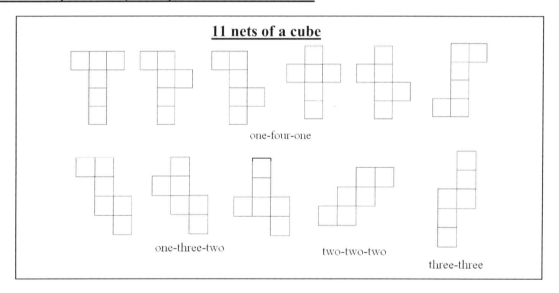

11 nets of a cube

one-four-one

one-three-two   two-two-two

three-three

Example 2: (2003 School Sprint) When this net of six squares is folded to make a cube, which face will be opposite face S?

Solution: Face C.

We draw red lines from points 1 and 2 to point O. Thus we know that faces E and D share the vertex with face S. We also know that face A is next to face S and face B shares vertex with S. So only face left is C which is the face opposite the face S.

Example 3: (1995 Mathcounts Chapter) Given the piece of paper that can be folded up to form a cube. What numbered face will be opposite the number 6 face?

Solution:

We draw red lines from points *A* and *B* to point *O*. Thus we know that face 2 and faces 4 and 6 share the vertex.
We draw red lines from points *C* and *D* to point *E*. Thus we know that faces 2 and 1 share the vertex with face 6 as well.
We also know that face 4 is next to face 6. So only face left is 3 which is the face opposite the face 6.

Example 4: (Mathcounts Competitions) When folded to form a cube, what is the value in the square opposite the one marked *x*?

Solution: 2.

We draw red lines from points A and B to point O. Thus we know that faces 1 and 3 share the vertex with face *x*.
We also know that faces 4 and 5 do not opposite face *x*. So only face left is 2 which

Example 5: (Mathcounts Competitions) The network of squares shown in the diagram is folded along the edges of the squares to form a cube. Which of the following is (are) views of the resulting cube?

Solution: (b) and (c).

We draw red lines from points 1, 2, and 3 to point *O*. Thus we know that faces A, B, and 6 F share the same vertex. So (c) is the resulting cube.
We also know that that faces C, D, and E share the same vertex. So (b) is also the resulting cube.

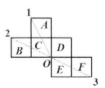

PROBLEMS

Problem 1: (2003 Mathcounts Chapter Sprint)The figure shown can be folded into the shape of a cube. In the resulting cube, which of the lettered faces is opposite the face marked x?

			D	E
		B	C	
x	A			

Problem 2: (Mathcounts) When folded to form a cube, what is the value in the square opposite the one marked x?

	2		
1	3	4	5
	x		

Problem 3: (2004 Mathcounts Chapter Sprint) This net is folded into a cube. When the cube is rolled, the *lateral product* is the product of the numbers on the four lateral faces. The numbers on the top and bottom faces are not included in the product. What is the greatest possible lateral product for this cube? 144

	1	
	3	4
	5	
2	6	

Problem 4: (2004 National Competition) When this net is folded to form a cube, which face (*A, B, C, D,* or *E*) will be opposite the face labeled "*S*"?

	A	S
C	B	
E	D	

Problem 5: (2003 Mathcounts Chapter Sprint) When this net of six squares is cut out and folded to form a cube, what is the product of the numbers on the four faces adjacent to the one labeled with a "1" ?

		1
	3	2
4	5	
	6	

SOLUTIONS

Problem 1: Solution: (C).

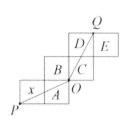

We select a point P and draw a line segment PO across two faces. We find another point which is Q as shown in the figure. We then know that P and Q will meet when folded. The face x will share the same vertex with the faces D and E, so D and E are not opposite to x. We also know that face x shares the same vertex with faces B and A. The only face left is face C, which must be opposite x.

Problem 2: Solution: 2.

Face 1 will touch face x and faces 3, 4, and 5 are adjacent to face x, so face 2 is opposite to face x in the folded cube.

Problem 3: Solution: 144.

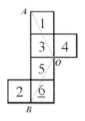

We draw red lines from points A and B to point O. Thus we know that faces 2 and 6 share the vertex with face 1. We also know that face 3 is next to face 1 and face 4 shares vertex with 1. So only face left is 5 which is the face opposite the face 1.

We put face 1 down and face 5 on the top after the cube is rolled in order to get the greatest possible lateral product, which is $2\times3\times4\times6 = 144$.

Problem 4: Solution: Face C.

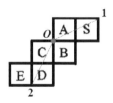

We draw red lines from points 1 and 2 to point O. Thus we know that faces E and D share the vertex with face S. We also know that face A is next to face S and face B shares vertex with S. So only face left is C which is the face opposite the face S.

Problem 5: Solution: 144.

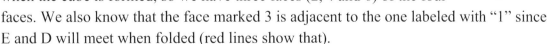

We know that face 2 is adjacent to face 1. We draw three black line segments as shown in the figure below.

From these line segments, we know that vertices A, B, and C will meet when the cube is formed, so we have three faces (2, 4 and 6) of the four faces. We also know that the face marked 3 is adjacent to the one labeled with "1" since E and D will meet when folded (red lines show that).

Therefore the product of the numbers on the four faces adjacent to the one labeled with a "1" is $2 \times 3 \times 4 \times 6 = 144$.

Example 1: Which vertices meet with vertex 1 when the net below is folded?

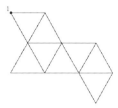

Step 1. Draw a line across **two triangular faces**, i.e. draw a line from the vertex 1 to point O.

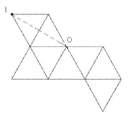

Step 2. Find other points that are the same distance to point O (in this case, find the points 2 and 3).

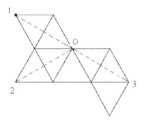

Step 3. Conclusion: Vertices 1, 2, and 3 will meet when the net is folded.

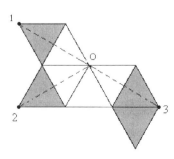

**Note that for an octahedron, four faces share one vertex.**

Net Of An Octahedron

An octahedron is the solid with six polyhedron vertices, twelve polyhedron edges, and eight equivalent equilateral triangular faces.

11 distinct nets for the octahedron.

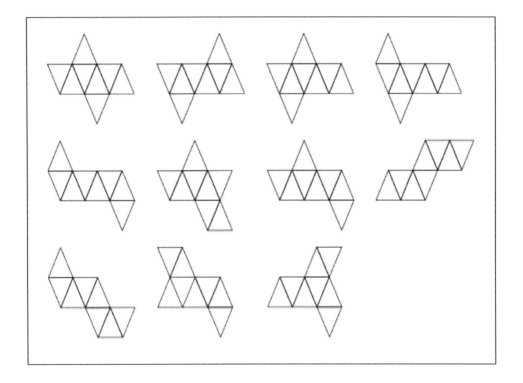

Example 2: (2004 Mathcounts State Sprint) This net is folded into a regular octahedron. What is the sum of the numbers on the triangular faces sharing an edge with the face with a "1" on it?

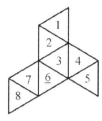

Solution: 14.

From the figure, it is easy to see that face 2 shares an edge with face 1. Now we just need to find the other two faces.

As shown in the figure and from our method, the faces are 8 and 4. (When folded, four faces 1, 4, 5, and 8 share one vertex. Note face 5 shares a vertex with face 1 but not an edge).

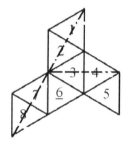

The sum of the three faces is $8 + 4 + 2 = 14$.

Example 3: (1994 Mathcounts National Competition) If the strip of triangles, as shown, is folded to form an octahedron, and each vertex is assigned the value of the sum of the four triangular faces to which it belongs, find the maximum value of a vertex.

Solution: 24.

We already know three faces that meet at vertex *A*: 8, 7, 6, so we only need to find one more face. Vertex *B* will meet Vertex *A* when folded, so the other face is the face marked "3". The faces marked with the numbers 8, 7, 6, and 3 form the maximum vertex. Answer: 24

PROBLEMS

Problem 1: Find the sum of the numbers on the triangular faces that share the same vertex as A.

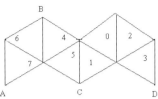

Problem 2: (Mathcounts) The net below can be folded up to form an octahedron. When it is folded up, which two vertices are glued to vertex V?

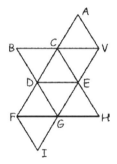

Problem 3: If the strip of triangles, as shown below, is folded to form an octahedron, and each vertex is assigned the value of the sum of the four triangular faces to which it belongs, find the minimum value of a vertex.

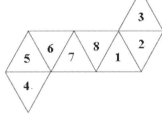

Problem 4: (Mathcounts) When the strip of triangles is folded to form an octahedron, which face is opposite the shaded one?

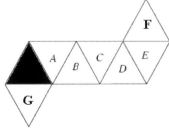

SOLUTIONS

Problem 1: Solution: 16.

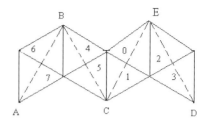

We know that one of the numbers is 7.
We see that *A* will meet with *C* and *D*.
So faces 7, 5, 1 and 3 share one vertex. The sum of the

values is 7 + 5 + 1 + 3 = 16.

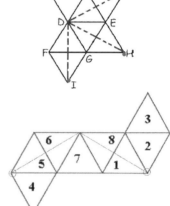

Problem 2: Solution: H, I.
The two vertices are *H* and *I*.

Problem 3: Solution: 12.
The minimum value is on the vertex with 1, 2, 4, and 5.
The sum is 12.

Problem 4: Solution: C.
The face that is opposite the shaded one should not share any vertices or edges with the shaded triangle.

We name the three vertices of the shaded triangle in the net *H*, *J*, and *K*. We draw line 1 from *K* to *P*. From this line, we draw line 2 based on our method in the chapter discussion. From line 2, we see that faces *D* and *E* share the same vertices with the shaded triangle.

Next, we draw line 3 from H to *Q* and we get line 4. From here, we know that face *F* shares a vertex with the shaded triangle.

 Looking at vertex *J*, we know that faces *A*, *G*, and *B* all share vertices with the shaded triangle. Therefore the only face not sharing any vertices or edges with the shaded triangle is face *C*.

Example 1: (2008 Mathcounts School Sprint) If only the positive integers from 1 through 49, inclusive, are written on a piece of paper, what is the sum of all the digits that are written on the paper?

Solution: 325.

Method 1: Note that $0 + 1 + 2 + 3 + 4 + 5 + 6 + 7 + 8 + 9 = 45$.

Referencing the table below, the sum of all the digits that are written on the paper from 1 to 49 is equal to

$5 \times 45 + 1 \times 10 + 2 \times 10 + 3 \times 10 + 4 \times 10 = 5 \times 45 + 10 \times (1 + 2 + 3 + 4)$
$= 5 \times 45 + 10 \times 10 = 325$.

0	10	20	30	40
1	11	21	31	41
2	12	22	32	42
3	13	23	33	43
4	14	24	34	44
5	15	25	35	45
6	16	26	36	46
7	17	27	37	47
8	18	28	38	48
9	19	29	39	49

Method 2:
Add a 0 and pair these numbers in such a way that $(0, 49), (1, 48), (2, 47), \ldots, (24, 25)$ form pairs.
The sum of the digits in each pair is 13 and we have 25 pairs, so the answer will be $13 \times 15 = 325$.

Note: Always add "0" and then divide the numbers into pairs like such: $(0, 99)$ or $(0, 199), \ldots, (0, 999)\ldots$ to avoid any mistakes.

Example 2: What is the sum of all the digits needed to write all the whole numbers from 1 to 199 inclusive?

Solution: 1900.

Add a 0 and group these numbers into 100 groups: $(0, 199), (1, 198)\ldots$

The sum of the digits in each group is 19, so the answer is 19 × 100= 1900.

Example 3: (Mathcounts 2004 State Target) The sum of all the digits used to write the whole numbers 10 through 13 is $1 + 0 + 1 + 1 + 1 + 2 + 1 + 3 = 10$. What is the sum of all the digits used to write the whole number 1 through 110, inclusive?

Solution: 957.

First we find the sum of all the digits from 0 to 99. We can group these 100 number into pairs to form the following pairs: (0, 99), (1, 98), (2, 97), (3, 96), …

In each pair, the sum of all the digits is 18. There are 50 pairs, so the sum of all the digits from 0 to 99 is $18 \times 50 = 900$.

Finding the sum of all the digits from 100 to 110 is simple. We have the numbers 100, 101, 102, 103, 104,105, 106, 107,108, 109, 110 which gives us the sum of all the digits as $1 \times 10 + (1 + 2 + 3 + … + 9) + 1 + 1 + 0 = 10 + 45 + 1 + 1 + 0 = 57$.

The sum of all the digits from 1 to 110 is $900 + 57 = 957$.
Note: The key point is to add "0" and to form the valid pairs.

Example 4: (Mathcounts 2000 National Team) What is the sum of the digits needed to write all the whole numbers from 0 to 10,000 inclusive?

Solution: 180,001.

We group the numbers from 0 to 9999 into pairs: (0, 9999), (1, 9998), (2, 9997),…
We must remember including number 10,000 in our final calculations.

There are 5,000 pairs and in each pair, the sum of all the digits is $4 \times 9 = 36$, so the sum of all the digits from 0 to 9999 is $36 \times 5000 = 180,000$.

The sum of the digits needed to write all the whole numbers from 0 to 10,000 inclusive equals $180,000 + 1$ (for 10,000) $= 180,001$.

PROBLEMS

Problem 1: If only the positive integers from 1 through 200, inclusive, are written on a piece of paper, what is the sum of all the digits that are written on the paper?

Problem 2: What is the sum of all the digits needed to write all the whole numbers from 1 to 499 inclusive?

Problem 3: The sum of all the digits used to write the whole numbers 10 through 13 is 1 + 0 + 1 + 1 + 1 + 2 + 1 + 3 = 10. What is the sum of all the digits used to write the whole number 1 through 310, inclusive?

Problem 4: What is the sum of the digits needed to write all the whole numbers from 0 to 1,000 inclusive?

Problem 5: If only the positive integers from 1 through 149, inclusive, are written on a piece of paper, what is the sum of all the digits that are written on the paper?

SOLUTIONS

Problem 1: Solution: 1902.

Add a 0 and pair these numbers in such a way that (0, 199), (1, 198), (2, 197), … , (99, 100) form pairs.

The sum of the digits in each pair is 19 and we have 100 pairs, so we get $19 \times 100 = 1900$.

Note we left the number 200 so the answer will be $1900 + 2 = 1902$.

Problem 2: Solution: 5500.

Method 1: Add a 0 and group these numbers into 250 groups: (0, 499), (1, 498)…

The sum of the digits in each group is 22, so the answer is $22 \times 250 = 5500$.

Problem 3: Solution: 3079.

Method 1:

First we find the sum of all the digits from 0 to 299. We can group these 300 number into pairs to form the following pairs: (0, 299), (1, 298), (2, 297), (3, 296), …, (149, 150).

In each pair, the sum of all the digits is 20. There are 150 pairs, so the sum of all the digits from 0 to 299 is $20 \times 150 = 3000$.

Finding the sum of all the digits from 300 to 310 is simple. We have the numbers 300, 301, 302, 303, 304, 305, 306, 307, 308, 309, 310 which gives us the sum of all the digits as $3 \times 10 + (1 + 2 + 3 + … + 9) + 3 + 1 + 0 = 30 + 45 + 3 + 1 + 0 = 79$.

The sum of all the digits from 1 to 110 is $3000 + 79 = 3079$.

Method 2:

If we add a 0 and pair these numbers directly like this: (0, 310), (1, 309), (2, 308),…, we are not able to get the same sum for each pair.

We first consider numbers from 0 to 309 and pair them up into two groups:

Group 1: (0, 309), (1, 308), (2, 307), … , (9, 300);
     (100, 209), (101, 208), (102, 207), … , (109, 200).
Group 2: (10, 299), (11, 298), …, (154, 155).

The sum of the digits for group 1 in each pair is 12 and we have 20 pairs, so we get $12 \times 20 = 240$.
The sum of the digits for group 2 in each pair is 21 and we have 135 pairs, so we get $21 \times 135 = 2835$.

Considering the number 310 which is left when we do out calculation, the answer will be $240 + 2835 + 3 + 1 = 3079$.

Problem 4: Solution: 13,501.

We group the numbers from 0 to 999 into pairs: $(0, 999), (1, 998), (2, 997),\ldots$
We must remember including number 1,000 in our final calculations.

There are 500 pairs and in each pair, the sum of all the digits is $3 \times 9 = 27$, so the sum of all the digits from 0 to 999 is $27 \times 500 = 13,500$.

The sum of the digits needed to write all the whole numbers from 0 to 1,000 inclusive equals $13,500 + 1$ (for 1000) $= 13,501$.

Problem 5: Solution: 1275.
Add a 0 and pair these numbers into two groups:
Group 1: $(0, 149), (1, 148), (2, 147), \ldots , (49, 100)$.
Group 2: $(50, 99), (51, 98), \ldots, (74, 75)$.

The sum of the digits for group 1 in each pair is 14 and we have 50 pairs, so we get $14 \times 50 = 700$.
The sum of the digits for group 2 in each pair is 23 and we have 25 pairs, so we get $23 \times 25 = 575$.

So the answer will be $700 + 575 = 1275$.

Example 1: (1997 Mathcounts Handbook) What is the sum of all five-digit permutations of 1, 3, 5, 7, and 9?

Solution: 6,666,600.

There are a total 5! = 120 such five-digit numbers. Each digit is used $120 \div 5 = 24$ times as a ten-thousand digit, thousands digit, a hundreds digit, a tens digit, and a units digit. The sum of all such five-digit positive integers is $24 \times (1 + 3 + 5 + 7 + 9) \times 11111 = 6,666,600$.

Sum of Numbers by Permutations of Digits

$$N = m\underbrace{(a_1 + a_2 + a_3 + \ldots + a_n)}_{n \text{ digits}}(\underbrace{111\ldots1}_{n \text{ 1's}})$$

m is the number of times each digit appears in the permutation of n digits.
$a_1, a_2, \ldots,$ and a_n are the digits.

Example 2: (2003 Mathcounts Chapter Sprint Round) What is the sum of all of the four-digit positive integers that can be written with the digits 1, 2, 3 and 4 if each digit must be used exactly once in each four-digit positive integer?

Solution: 66660.

There are a total 4! = 24 such four-digit numbers. Each digit is used $24 \div 4 = 6$ times as a thousands digit, a hundreds digit, a tens digit, and a units digit.

The sum of all such four-digit positive integers is $6 \times (1 + 2 + 3 + 4) \times 1111 = 66,660$.

Example 3: Find the sum of all two-digit positive integers if each digit must be used exactly once in each two-digit positive integer.

Solution:

Method 1:
(1). We first find the sum of all two-digit positive integers formed by the digits 1 to 9. We have $9 \times 8 = 72$ two-digit positive integers. Each digit is used $72 \div 9 = 8$ times as a tens digit, and a units digit.
$$N = m\underbrace{(a_1 + a_2 + a_3 + \ldots + a_n)}_{n \text{ digits}}(\underbrace{111\ldots1}_{n \text{ 1's}}) = 8 \times (1 + 2 + 3 + \ldots + 9) \times 11 = 3960.$$

(2). We then find the sum of all two-digit positive integers with the units digit of 0.
$10 + 20 +...+ 90 = 10(1 + 2 + 3+...+ 9) = 10 \times 45 = 450$.
The final answer is $3960 + 450 = 4410$.

Method 2:
(1). We first find the sum of all two-digit "codes" formed by the digits 0 to 9.
We have $10 \times 9 = 90$ such two-digit "codes". Each digit is used $90 \div 10 = 9$ times as a tens digit and a units digit.

Each digit is used $90/10 = 9$ times.
$$N = m(\underbrace{a_1 + a_2 + a_3 +...+ a_n}_{n \text{ digits}})(\underbrace{111...1}_{n \text{ 1's}}) = 9 \times (0 + 1 + 2 + 3 +...+ 9) \times 11 = 99 \times 45.$$

(2). We then find the sum of all two-digit "codes" with the tens digit of 0. These "codes" are not two-digit positive integers (like 01 or 03).
$01 + 02 +...+ 09 = 1 + 2 + 3 +...+ 9 = 45$.
The final answer is $99 \times 45 - 45 = 98 \times 45 = 4410$.

Example 4: (2004 Mathcounts Chapter Sprint) Cammy made a list of every possible distinct five-digit positive even integer that can be formed using each of the digits 1, 3, 4, 5 and 9 exactly once in each integer. What is the sum of the integers on Cammy's list?

Solution: 1199976.

Because the integers formed need to be even, the last digit of every number can only be 4.
If we leave the units digit (that is the digit 4) out, we can just calculate the sum of the four-digit numbers formed by 1, 3, 5, and 9, multiply the result by 10, and then add 4×24 to get the final answer.
1, 3, 5, and 9 will form $4! = 24$ four-digit integers. The number of digits used to make these 24 numbers is $24 \times 4 = 96$ including the digits 1, 3, 5, and 9.

So each digit is used $96 \div 4 = 24$ times. Since each digit is evenly used in the formation of four-digit numbers, so each digit is used the same number of times.

In this case, each digit is used $24 \div 4 = 6$ times as a thousands digit, a hundreds digit, a tens digit, and a units digit.

The sum of these integers will be $6(1+3+5+9) \times 1111 = 119988$
$119988 \times 10 = 1199880$.
The sum of the integers on Cammy's list is $1199880 + 4 \times 24 = 1199976$.

PROBLEMS

Problem 1: What is the sum of all five-digit permutations of 1, 2, 3, 4, and 5?

Problem 2: Find the sum of all 4-digit positive integers formed by permuting 1, 2, 2, and 5.

Problem 3: Find the sum of all 3-digit positive integers formed by permuting 1, 2, 2, and 5.

Problem 4: (2003 Mathcounts Handbook Warm Up) What is the sum of all the elements of all the subsets containing exactly three different elements from the set {1, 2, 3, 4, 5, 6}?

Problem 5: (Mathcounts 1994 National Team) Five different digits are selected at random from the digits 1 through 9. S is the sum of all possible four-digit numbers that can be created by using these four digits. F is the greatest common factor of all such sums. Find F.

SOLUTIONS

Problem 1: Solution: 3,999,960.

There are a total 5! = 120 such five-digit numbers. Each digit is used 120 ÷ 5 = 24 times as a ten-thousand digit, thousands digit, a hundreds digit, a tens digit, and a units digit. The sum of all such five-digit positive integers is $24 \times (1 + 2 + 3 + 4 + 5) \times 11111 =$ 3,999,960.

Problem 2: Solution:

There are $\dfrac{4!}{2!} = 12$ such 4-digit positive integers. Each digit is used $m = \dfrac{12}{4} = 3$ times.

The sum of all these 4-digit positive integers is
$$N = m(\underbrace{a_1 + a_2 + a_3 + \ldots + a_n}_{n \text{ digits}})(\underbrace{111\ldots1}_{n \text{ 1's}}) = 3 \times (1 + 2 + 2 + 5) \times 1111 = 33330.$$

Problem 3: Solution: 3330.

There are 6 permutations with the digits 1, 2, and 5. There are 3 permutations with the digits 1, 2, and 2. There are 3 permutations with the digits 5, 2, and 2. So we have 12 such 3-digit positive integers total.

Each digit is used $m = \dfrac{12}{4} = 3$ times.

The sum of all these 4-digit positive integers is
$$N = m(\underbrace{a_1 + a_2 + a_3 + \ldots + a_n}_{n \text{ digits}})(\underbrace{111\ldots1}_{n \text{ 1's}}) = 3 \times (1 + 2 + 2 + 5) \times 111 = 3330.$$

Problem 4: Solution: 210.

There are $\dbinom{6}{3} = 20$ ways to choose three items from a group of six, so there are 20 subsets containing three elements. This means that if you were to write out all 20 subsets, you would write 60 numbers. Each of the elements in the original set would be used an equal amount of times, so each of the six original elements occurs $\dfrac{20 \times 3}{6} = 10$ times. The sum of all the elements of the 20 subsets is then $10 \times (1 + 2 + 3 + 4 + 5 + 6) = 210$.

Notes: This question is similar to "find the sum of all three-digit positive integers formed by using digits 1, 2, 3, 4, 5, and 6 without repetition."
 The difference in this problem is that the position value of each digit is ignored.
For example, "3" in number 345 is only "3", not "300".
We also need to note that "{3, 4, 5}" forms 1 subset. No further permutation is needed.

Problem 5: Solution: 6666.

We start from a simple case. Assume we select 1, 2, 3, and 4, then the total numbers of 4-digit numbers will be $4 \times 3 \times 2 \times 1$. Each digit is used $4 \times 3 \times 2 \times 1 / 4$ times as a thousands digit, a hundreds digit, a tens digit, and a units digit.

The sum of all these numbers will be

$$S_1 = \frac{4 \times 3 \times 2 \times 1}{4} \times (1 + 2 + 3 + 4)(1000 + 100 + 10 + 1) = 6666 \times (1 + 2 + 3 + 4)$$

If we select the digits 2, 3,4, and 5, we have

$$S_2 = \frac{4 \times 3 \times 2 \times 1}{4} \times (2 + 3 + 4 + 5)(1000 + 100 + 10 + 1) = 6666 \times (2 + 3 + 4 + 5)$$

Similarly, we have

$$S_3 = \frac{4 \times 3 \times 2 \times 1}{4} \times (3 + 4 + 5 + 6)(1000 + 100 + 10 + 1) = 6666 \times (3 + 4 + 5 + 6)$$

....

$$S_n = \frac{4 \times 3 \times 2 \times 1}{4} \times (a_1 + a_2 + a_3 + a_4)(1000 + 100 + 10 + 1) = 6666 \times (a_1 + a_2 + a_3 + a_4)$$

So the greatest common factor will be 6666.

Example 1: (2000 Mathcounts Handbook) Tim and Kurt are playing a game in which players are awarded either 3 points or 7 points for a correct answer. What is the greatest score that cannot be attained?

Solution: 11.

Method 1:
By the formula, m = 7 and n = 3.
The highest score you cannot get is m × n – (m + n) = 7 × 3 – (7 + 3) = 21 – 10 = 11.

Method 2:
We are able to get 10 = 7 + 3. But we are not able to get 11.
Any number can be written as one of the forms:
$3m$ (m is positive integer)
$3m + 1$ (m is nonnegative integer)
$3m + 2$ (m is nonnegative integer)

For any number greater than 11, $m \geq 4$. So $m - 4$ is nonnegative number.

If a number is in the form of $3m$, it is attainable by using m 3's.
If a number is in the form of $3m + 1$, $3m + 1 = 7 + 3m - 6 = 7 + 3(m - 2)$, which is attainable by using one 7 and $(m - 2)$ 3's.
If a number is in the form of $3m + 2$, $3m + 2 = 14 + 3m - 12 = 7 \times 2 + 3(m - 4)$, which is attainable by using two 7's and $(m - 4)$ 3's.

We see that all numbers are covered by the combinations of 7 and 3. So we are sure that 11 is the greatest number that cannot be attained.

> **The maximum number not attained by a combination of two natural numbers**
> ***m*** **and** ***n*** **is** ***m*** **×** ***n*** **– (*m* + *n*).** ***m*** **and** ***n*** **are relatively prime.**

Example 2: Jarrett can buy erasers in quantities of 3 and 8. What is the largest number of erasers that Jarrett cannot buy?

Solution: 13.

Method 1:
By the formula, $3 \times 8 - 3 - 8 = 13$.

Method 2:
We are able to get $8 + 3 = 11$ and $3 \times 4 = 12$. But we are not able to get 13. We are able to get $8 + 3 + 3 = 14$.
Any number can be written as one of the forms:
$3m$ (m is positive integer)
$3m + 1$ (m is nonnegative integer)
$3m + 2$ (m is nonnegative integer)

For any integer greater than 14, $m \geq 5$. So $m - 5$ is positive integer.
If a number is in the form of $3m$, it is attainable by using m 3's.
If a number is in the form of $3m + 1$, $3m + 1 = 16 + 3m - 15 = 8 \times 2 + 3(m - 5)$, which is attainable by using two 8's and $(m - 3)$ 3's.
If a number is in the form of $3m + 2$, $3m + 2 = 8 + 3m - 2 = 8 + 3(m - 2)$, which is attainable by using one 8 and $(m - 2)$ 3's.

We see that all numbers are covered by the combinations of 8 and 3. So we are sure that 13 is the greatest number that cannot be attained.

Example 3: (Mathcounts) Julian has weights of 1, 3, and 7 pounds. What is the smallest whole number of pounds he cannot weigh using these three weights and a balance scale?

Solution: 12 pounds.

He cannot weigh 12 pounds because $1 + 3 + 7 = 11$.
We need to make sure no other smaller number of pounds that he cannot weigh.
He can weigh 1 pound.
If he put 3 pounds weight on one side and 1 pound weight on other side of the scale, he can weigh 2 pounds.
We see $1 + 3 = 4$, $1 + 7 - 3 = 5$, $6 = 7 - 1$, $1 + 7 = 8$, $7 + 3 - 1 = 9$, $7 + 3 = 10$.
So we are sure that 12 is the smallest whole number of pounds he cannot weigh.

Example 4: In a certain football league, the only way to score is to kick a field goal for 3 points or score a touchdown for 7 points. Thus the scores 1, 4 and 8 are not possible. How many positive scores are not possible?

Solution: 6.

Method 1:
One checks directly that the following list of scores up to 14 is the complete list of obtainable scores up to that point: 3, 6, 7, 9, 10, 12, 13, 14. Now, we have 3 consecutive scores, namely 12, 13, and 14, which are obtainable, and this implies every score > 14 is obtainable. To see this, observe that if n is an obtainable score, then so is n + 3 (simply add another field goal to whatever it took to get n points); hence, 15 = 12 + 3, 16 = 13 + 3, and 17 = 14 + 3 are all obtainable and so are 18 = 15 + 3, 19 = 16 + 3, 20 = 17 + 3, and so on. Therefore, the positive integral scores which are not obtainable are 1, 2, 4, 5, 8, and 11. Thus, the answer is 6.

Method 2: By formula, the maximum number that cannot be obtained is $3 \times 7 - 3 - 7 = 11$. So we have 1, 2, 4, 5, 8, and 11, all these 6 scores are not obtainable.

PROBLEMS

Problem 1: (Mathcounts) What is the highest score you cannot get on the dart board shown below if you may use as many darts as you wish?

Problem 2: In a village the only currency is 7-cent and 11-cent coins. Some prices such as 42, can be paid with exact change, while others, like 5 or 20 cannot. How many prices can not be paid with exact change?
(A) 28   (B) 29   (C) 30   (D) 31   (E) None of above

Problem 3: Tim and Kurt are playing a game in which players are awarded either 3 points or 10 points for a correct answer. What is the greatest score that cannot be attained?

Problem 4: (1998 Mathcounts National) A science test has 10 questions worth 5 points each, 7 questions worth 6 points each, and 4 questions worth 2 points each. None of these questions will be given partial credit. How many scores between 0 and 100 are impossible to score?

Problem 5: Chicken McNuggets come in packages of size 6, 9 and 20. What is the largest number of McNuggets which cannot be purchased?

Problem 6: (2006 Mathcounts Chapter) Eli throws five darts at a circular target, and each one lands within one of the four regions. The point-value of a dart landing in each region is indicated. What is the least score greater than five points that is *not* possible when the point values of the five darts are added together?

SOLUTIONS

Problem 1: Solution: 23.

By the formula, $m = 9$ and $n = 4$.

The highest score you cannot get is $m \times n - (m + n) = 9 \times 4 - (9 + 4) = 36 - 13 = 23$.

Problem 2: Solution: 30.

We know that the greatest value that cannot be paid is

$7 \times 11 - (7 + 11) = 59$

For $7n$, we have

$7n < 59 \Rightarrow \quad n < 8.4 \qquad \Rightarrow n$ has 8 values (from 1 to 8).

(7, 14, 21, 28, 35, 42, 49, 56)

For $11m$, we have

$11m < 59 \Rightarrow m < 5.3 \qquad \Rightarrow m$ has 5 values (from 1 to 5).

(11, 22, 33, 44, 55)

For $7n + 11m$, we have

$7n + 11m < 59$

Case I: $m = 1$

$7n < 59 - 11 = 48 \qquad \Rightarrow \qquad n < 6.8 \Rightarrow n$ has 6 values (from 1 to 6).

Similarly:

Case II: $m = 2 \Rightarrow \qquad n$ has 5 values.

Case III: $m = 3 \qquad \Rightarrow \qquad n$ has 3 values.

Case III: $m = 4 \qquad \Rightarrow \qquad n$ has 2 values.

Note when $m = 5$, there is not integer value for n.

Total $8 + 5 + 6 + 5 + 3 + 2 = 29$ values possible.

There are $59 - 29 = 30$ prices that cannot be paid.

Problem 3: Solution: 17.

Method 1:

By the formula, $m = 10$ and $n = 3$.

The highest score you cannot get is $m \times n - (m + n) = 10 \times 3 - (10 + 3) = 30 - 13 = 17$.

Method 2:

We are able to get $10 + 3 + 3 = 16$. But we are not able to get 17.

Any number can be written as one of the forms:

$3m$ (m is positive integer)

$3m + 1$ (m is nonnegative integer)

$3m + 2$ (m is nonnegative integer)

For any number greater than 17, $m \geq 6$. So $m - 6$ is nonnegative number.

If a number is in the form of $3m$, it is attainable by using m 3's.
If a number is in the form of $3m + 1$, $3m + 1 = 10 + 3m - 9 = 10 + 3(m - 3)$, which is attainable by using one 10 and $(m - 3)$ 3's.
If a number is in the form of $3m + 2$, $3m + 2 = 20 + 3m - 18 = 20 + 3(m - 6)$, which is attainable by using two 10's and $(m - 6)$ 3's.

We see that all numbers are covered by the combinations of 10 and 3. So we are sure that 17 is the greatest number that cannot be attained.

Problem 4: Solution: 4 scores (1, 3, 97, 99).
We have $100 = 10 \times 5 + 7 \times 6 + 4 \times 2$.
When we miss questions with 2 points, at most we can get a 98, 96, 94,...
We are not able to get a 99.
When we miss questions with 5 points, at most we can get a 95.
We are not able to get a 97.
From the lower side, we are not able to get 1 and 3.
We guess that that is all we are not able to get.

Any number between 6 and 96 will be able to get:

$6k$: the greatest value is 96. $96 = 6 \times 7 + 5 \times 10 + 2 \times 2 = 6 \times 7 + 5 \times (6 + 4) + 2 \times 2 = 6 \times 7 + 6 \times 5 + 5 \times 4 + 4 = = 6 \times 7 + 6 \times 5 + 6 \times 4$

$6k + 1$: the greatest value is 91. $91 = 6 \times 7 + 5 \times 9 + 2 \times 2 = 6 \times 7 + 5 \times 6 + 5 \times 3 + 2 \times 2 = 6 \times 7 + 6 \times 5 + 6 \times 3 + 1$

$6k + 2$: the greatest value is 98. $98 = 6 \times 7 + 5 \times 10 + 3 \times 2 = 6 \times 7 + 5 \times (6 + 4) + 3 \times 2 = 6 \times 7 + 5 \times 6 + 20 + 3 \times 2 = 6 \times 7 + 5 \times 6 + 6 \times 3 + 6 + 2$

$6k + 3$: the greatest value is 93. $93 = 6 \times 7 + 5 \times 9 + 3 \times 2 = 6 \times 7 + 5 \times (6 + 3) + 6 = 6 \times 7 + 5 \times 6 + 5 \times 3 + 6 = 6 \times 7 + 5 \times 6 + 6 + 6 \times 3 + 3$

$6k + 4$: the greatest value is 94. $94 = 6 \times 7 + 5 \times 10 + 2 = 6 \times 7 + 5 \times (6 + 4) + 2 = 6 \times 7$

$+ 5 \times 6 + 20 + 2 = = 6 \times 7 + 5 \times 6 + 6 \times 3 + 4$

$6k + 5$: the greatest value is 95. $95 = 6 \times 7 + 5 \times 9 + 4 \times 2 = 6 \times 7 + 5 \times (6 + 3) + 4 \times 2 = 6 \times 7 + 6 \times 5 + 6 \times 2 + 3 + 6 + 2 = 6 \times 7 + 6 \times 5 + 6 \times 2 + 6 + 5$.

Problem 5: Solution: 43.
We are able to get 40, $42 = 9 \times 4 + 6$, $44 = 20 + 6 \times 4$, and $45 = 9 \times 5$. We are not able to get 41 and 43.

Since we want to find the largest possible number, we guess that the answer is 43.

Any number can be written as one of the forms:
$6m$ (m is positive integer)
$6m + 1$ (m is nonnegative integer)
$6m + 2$ (m is nonnegative integer)
$6m + 3$ (m is nonnegative integer)
$6m + 4$ (m is nonnegative integer)
$6m + 5$ (m is nonnegative integer)

For any number greater than 43, $m \geq 7$. So $m - 7$ is nonnegative number.

If a number is in the form of 6m, it is attainable.

If a number is in the form of $6m + 1$, $6m + 1 = 81 + 6m - 80 = 9 \times 9 + 6m - 20 \times 4$, which is attainable.

If a number is in the form of $6m + 2$, $6m + 2 = 20 + 6m - 18 = 20 + 6(m - 3)$, which is attainable by using one 20 and ($m - 3$) 6's.

If a number is in the form of $6m + 3$, $6m + 3 = 9 + 6m - 6 = 9 + 6(m - 1)$, which is attainable by using one 9 and ($m - 1$) 6's.

If a number is in the form of $6m + 4$, $6m + 4 = 40 + 6m - 36 = 40 + 6(m - 6)$, which is attainable by using two 20's and ($m - 6$) 6's.

If a number is in the form of $6m + 5$, $6m + 5 = 20 + 9 + 6m - 24 = 20 + 9 + 6(m - 4)$, which is attainable by using one 20, one 9, and $(m - 4)$ 6's.

We see that all numbers are covered by the combinations of 6, 9, and 20. So we are sure that 43 is the greatest number that cannot be attained.

Problem 6: Solution: 27.
At most the score can be $6 + 6 + 6 + 6 + 6 = 30$. So we are not able to make 31. We do a little more calculations:
$6 + 6 + 6 + 6 + 4 = 28$.
$6 + 6 + 6 + 6 + 2 = 26$.
$6 + 6 + 6 + 6 + 1 = 25$.
We see that we are not able to make 29 and 27.

Since we want to find the least possible number, we guess that 27 is the answer.
Now we verify our guess:

A	B	C	D	E	Sum
2	1	1	1	1	6

By adding 1 to B, C, D, E, successively, we are able to get the sum of 7, 8, 9, or 10, respectively.

A	B	C	D	E	Sum
6	1	1	1	1	10

By adding 1 to B, C, D, E, successively, we are able to get the sum of 11, 12, 13, or 14.

A	B	C	D	E	Sum
6	6	1	1	1	15

By adding 1 to C, D, E, successively, we are able to get the sum of 16, 17, or 18. By adding 4 to C, 2 to D, we are able to get a sum of 19.

A	B	C	D	E	Sum
6	6	6	1	1	20

By adding 1 to D, and E, successively, we are able to get the sum of 21 or 22. When we add 4 to D, we get 23, and then we get the sum of 24 by adding 1 to E.
So we see that we are able to get all. The answer is indeed 27.

Example 1: In how many ways can 5 be written as the sum of three positive integers? Note: $1 + 1 + 3$ and $1 + 3 + 1$ are counted as different ways.

Solution: 6.

Method 1:

We write out all the combinations:

$5 = 1 + 1 + 3 = 1 + 3 + 1 = 3 + 1 + 1 = 1 + 2 + 2 = 2 + 1 + 2 = 2 + 2 + 1$

Since order matters, there are 6 ways to do so.

Method 2:

We put 5 1's as follows:

1   1   1   1   1

We put one partition between any two numbers.

1 | 1 | 1 | 1 | 1

Since we want to have three numbers, we need two partitions. The following figure shows $5 = 1 + 3 + 1$.

1 | 1   1   1 | 1

We have a total of 4 partitions but we only need two every time.

So we have $\binom{4}{2} = 6$ ways to write 5 as the sum of three positive integers.

If n is a natural number, the number of ways it can be written as the sum of m natural numbers if order matters ($n > m$) is $\binom{n-1}{m-1}$.

Example 2: There are 8 identical soccer balls to be given to 4 boys. Each boy needs to get at least one ball. How many ways to distribute the balls?

Solution:

Put 8 balls in a row. There are 7 spaces among the balls.

We want to divide them into 4 groups, that is to use 3 partitions. The following figure shows an example of the division $8 = 1 + 2 + 2 + 3$.

We have 7 partitions but we only need 3 every time. So we have $\binom{7}{3} = 35$ ways.

Example 3: Positive integer 3 can be expressed in different ways: $3, 1 + 2, 2 + 1, 1 + 1 + 1$. How many ways to express the number 11?

Solution: 2^{10}.

We can write the number 3 as three 1's: 1 1 1 in a row. We see two spaces between these three 1's. We have two choices: (1) fill a space with "+" sign, or (2) leave it blank. Then we get 2^2 ways to express the number 3. For the number 11, we can write 11 1's in a row and make 10 spaces between the 1's. Therefore we have 2^{10} ways to express the number 11.

> If n is a natural number, the number of ways it can be expressed as the sum of one or more natural numbers if order matters is 2^{n-1}.

Example 4: Write the number 11 as the sum of five natural numbers. What is the greatest product of them?

Solution: 48.

In order to get the greatest product we must make any two numbers equal or their difference is 1. $11 = 5 \times 2 + 1 = 2 + 2 + 2 + 2 + 2 + 1 = 2 + 2 + 2 + 2 + 3$. The greatest product will be $2^4 \times 3 = 48$.

If natural number $S = pq + r$ $(0 \le r \le p$, p and q are natural numbers), S can be written as the sum of p natural numbers and the product of these p numbers has the greatest value M, and $M = q^{p-r} \times (q+1)^r$.

Example 5: Write 14 as the sum of two or more natural numbers and to get the greatest value of the product of the numbers.

Solution:

$14 = 3 + 3 + 3 + 3 + 2$.
The greatest product will be $M = 3^4 \times 2 = 162$.

$S = a_1 + a_2 + a_3 + \ldots + a_n$. The product of a_1, a_2, a_3, $\ldots$, a_n has the greatest value only when there are at most two 2's among a_1, a_2, a_3, $\ldots$, a_n, and the rest are 3's.

Example 6: (2012 Mathcounts State) In how many ways can 18 be written as the sum of four distinct positive integers? Note: $1 + 3 + 5 + 9$ and $5 + 1 + 3 + 9$ are counted as different ways.

Solution: 360.

The number of ways to express 18 as the sum of 4 positive integers is $\binom{17}{3} = 680$.

We have the following cases that are not working:

Three positive integers are the same: $3a + b = 18$ (1)
Two positive integers are the same: $2a + b + c = 18$ (2)
$$2a + 2b = 18 \qquad (3)$$
For equation (1), we have 5 solutions of (a, b): (5, 15), (4, 6), (3, 9), (2, 14), and (1, 12).
Then we have $5 \times 4!/3! = 20$ ways.

For equation (2), we have 23 solutions:

a	$b + c$	solutions
7	4	1
6	6	2
5	8	2
4	10	3
3	12	4
2	14	5
1	16	6
Total		23

Then we have $23 \times 4!/2! = 23 \times 12 = 276$ ways.

For equation (3), we have $a + b = 9$ with 4 solutions of (a, b): (1, 8), (2, 7), (3, 6), and (4, 5).
Then we have $4 \times 4!/2!2! = 24$ ways.

Our answer is $680 - 20 - 276 - 24 = 360$.

PROBLEMS

Problem 1: In how many ways can 10 be written as the sum of 7 positive integers? Note: $1 + 1 + 1 + 1 + 1 + 1 + 4$ and $1 + 1 + 1 + 1 + 1 + 4 + 1$ are counted as different ways.

Problem 2: Positive integer 3 can be expressed in different ways: $3, 1 + 2, 2 + 1, 1 + 1 + 1$. How many ways to express the number 1999?

Problem 3: Write the number 1999 as the sum of eight natural numbers. What is the greatest product of them?

Problem 4: Write 19 as the sum of two or more natural numbers. What is the greatest value of the product of these numbers?

Problem 5: In how many ways can 12 be written as the sum of three distinct positive integers? Note: $1 + 3 + 8$ and $1 + 8 + 3$ are counted as different ways.

SOLUTIONS

Problem 1: Solution: 6.

We put 10 1's as follows:

1 ▌ 1 ▌ 1 ▌ 1 ▌ 1 ▌ 1 ▌ 1 ▌ 1 ▌ 1 ▌ 1

We put six parturitions between any two numbers.

1 ▌ 1   1   1   1 ▌ 1 ▌ 1 ▌ 1 ▌ 1 ▌ 1

Since we want to have three numbers, we need two partitions. The above figure shows 10 = 1 + 4 + 1 + 1 + 1 + 1 + 1.

We have s total of 9 partitions but we only need six every time.

So we have $\binom{9}{6} = \binom{9}{3} = 84$ ways to write 10 as the sum of seven positive integers.

Problem 2: Solution: 2^{1998}.
We can write the number 3 as three 1's: 1 1 1 in a row. We see two spaces between these three 1's. We have two choices: (1) fill a space with "+" sign, or (2) leave it blank. Then we get 2^2 ways to express the number 3. For the number 1999, we can write 1999 1's in a row and make 1998 spaces between the 1's. Therefore we have 2^{1998} ways to express the number 1999.

Problem 3: Solution: $250^7 \times 249$.
Method 1:
In order to get the greatest product we must make any two numbers equal or their difference is 1.

$1999 = 8 \times 249 + 7 = (249 + 1) + (249 + 1) + (249 + 1) + (249 + 1) + (249 + 1) + (249 + 1) + (249 + 1) + 249$.
The greatest product will be $250^7 \times 249$.

Method 2:

$1999 = 8 \times 249 + 7$.

The greatest value is $M = q^{p-r} \times (q+1) = 249^{8-7} \times (249+1)^7 = 249 \times 250^7$.

Problem 4: Solution: 972.

$19 = 3 + 3 + 3 + 3 + 3 + 2 + 2$.

The greatest product will be $M = 3^5 \times 2^2 = 972$.

Problem 5: Solution: 43.

Method 1:

We can write out all in an organized way:

$1 + 2 + 9;$ $1 + 3 + 8;$ $1 + 4 + 7;$ $1 + 5 + 6$

$2 + 3 + 7;$ $2 + 4 + 6$

$3 + 4 + 5.$

Each expression will generate $3! = 6$ ways.

Total we have $7 \times 6 = 42$ ways.

Method 2:

The number of ways to express 12 as the sum of 3 positive integers is $\binom{11}{2} = 55$.

We have the following cases that are not working:

Case I: Three positive integers are the same: $a + a + 3 = 3a = 12$.

We have one way for this: $12 = 4 + 4 + 4$.

Case II: Two positive integers are the same: $a + a + b = 2a + b = 12$.

At most $a = 5$ and at least $a = 1$. So we have 5 pairs of (a, b): (5, 2), (4, 4), (3, 6), (2, 8), and (1, 10).

Note that (4, 4) was counted in case I.

Each pair of (a, b) will generate an expression of 12, for example, with (5, 2), we have $12 = 5 + 5 + 2$.

For each expression, we have $3!/2! = 3$ ways (for examples, $5 + 5 + 2$, $5 + 2 + 5$, and $2 + 5 + 5$).

Thus we have $4 \times 3 = 12$ ways. Our answer is $55 - 1 - 12 = 42$.

Example 1: How many different line segments can be obtained for the following figure?

Solution: 21.

Two points will form a line. The solution will be: $\binom{n}{2} = \binom{6}{2} = 15$ line segments.

Example 2: What is the sum of the lengths of all segments in the figure below if the letters are equally-spaced with $AB = 1$.

Solution: 21.

Method 1:

There are $\binom{6}{2} = 15$ line segments. When we count these segments, we count $5AB + 8BC + 9CD + 8DE + 5EF = 35$.

Method 2:

$$a_1(n-1)\times 1 + a_2(n-2)\times 2 + a_3(n-3)\times 3 + \ldots + a_{n-1}\times 1 \times (n-1)$$
$$= 1\times(6-1)\times 1 + 1\times(6-2)\times 2 + 1\times(6-3)\times 3 + \ldots + 1\times 1\times(6-1) = 35.$$

Example 3: How many rays can be formed?

Solution: 10.

Each point will generate 2 rays (opposite directions). Five points can form 10 rays.

> The number of line segments can be formed with n points is $\binom{n}{2}$.

> Number of rays can be formed with n points is $2n$.

> The total length of the segments is number of line segments can be formed with n points is
> $$a_1(n-1)\times 1 + a_2(n-2)\times 2 + a_3(n-3)\times 3 + ... + a_{n-1}\times 1\times(n-1).$$
> a_i is the length of the segments, where $i = 1, 2, ..., n-1$.

Example 4: How many non-overlap lines can be drawn through 16 point in the figure?

Solution:

The total lines (regardless overlapping) is $\binom{16}{2}=120$. But we can only draw one non-overlap line through any five points on each side.

The desired solution is $\binom{16}{2} - 4\binom{5}{2} + 4 = 120 - 40 + 4 = 84$.

Example 5: A ruler with the length of 13 cm has no marks on it. How many marks need to be put on the ruler so that it can be used to measure all the lengths from 1 cm to 13 cm?

Solution:

We need two marks to do any measurement.

We need to get $\binom{n+2}{n} = 13$.

n is the number of marks that need to be put, 2 counts for two end points of the ruler when marked n marks.

We know $\binom{5}{3} = 10$, so 3 marks are not enough.

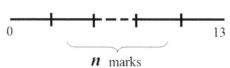

n marks

$\binom{6}{4}$ = 15. We need to put 4 marks. For example, 1, 4, 5, 11 will suffice. 1, 13 − 11 = 2, 4 − 1 = 3, 4, 5, 11 − 5 = 6, 11 − 4 = 7, 13 − 5 = 8, 13 − 4 = 9, 11 − 1 = 10, 11, 13 − 1 = 12, and 13. Note: 1, 2, 6, and 10 are also Okay.

Example 6: How many segments are determined by 9 points as shwon in the figure?

Solution:

Method 1:

We select one point from the top line and one point from the bottom line to form $\binom{4}{1} \times \binom{5}{1}$ = 20 segments.

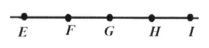

Method 2:

We have total 9 points and at most we can form $\binom{9}{2}$ segments. But any two points selected from from the top line will noe be able to form a segment. Simialrly for 5 points from the bottom line.

The number of segments that can be formed is $\binom{9}{2} - \binom{4}{2} - \binom{5}{2} = 20$.

PROBLEMS

Problem 1: (Mathcounts) How many different line segments coluld be named from the diagram?

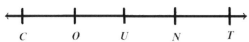

Problem 2: (Mathcounts) (rays) How many rays are determined by 4 points on a line?

Problem 3: (Mathcounts) Thirteen points have been placed in a plane so that no three points are cooinear. What is the number of different lines determined by these points?

Problem 4: (Mathcounts) Seven distinct points of a circle are chosen. How many line segments are ditermined by these points?

Problem 5: (Mathcounts) How many points, no three of which are collinear, determine 36 lines?

Problem 6: How many line segments can be counted in the figure? Note that a dot is an endpoint of segment.

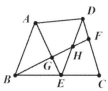

Problem 7: Four points are arranged on a plane such that the number of lines can be determined by them is n. Find sum of all possible values of n.

SOLUTIONS

Problem 1: Solution: 10.

Two points will form a line. The solution will be: $\binom{n}{2} = \binom{5}{2} = 10$ line segments.

Problem 2: Solution: 8.
Each point will generate 2 rays (opposite directions). Four points can form 8 rays.

Problem 3: Solution: 78.

Two points will form a line. The solution will be: $\binom{n}{2} = \binom{13}{2} = 78$ line segments.

Problem 4: Solution: 21 (segments).

Since no three of the seven points are collinear, we get at most $\binom{7}{2} = 21$ lines.

Problem 5: Solution: 9 (points).
Let the number of points be n.

We have $\binom{n}{2} = 36 \quad \Rightarrow \quad n(n-1) = 72 = 8 \times 9 \quad \Rightarrow \quad n = 9.$

Problem 6: Solution: 20.
Method 1:
AB, AG, AE, AD.
BG, BH, BF, BE, BC.
CD, CF, CE.
DE, DH, DF.
EG, EH.
We get $4 + 5 + 3 + 3 + 2 + 2 + 1 = 20$.

Method 2:

We get at most $\binom{8}{2} = 28$ line segment from eight points.

But we are not able to count *AF, AH, AC, BD, EF, CH, CG*, and *DG*. $28 - 8 = 20$.

Problem 7: Solution: 11.
The minimum number of lines can be determined by four points on the same plan is 1 if the four points are collinear.

The maximum number of lines can be determined by four points on the same plan is $\binom{4}{2} = 6$ 1 if no three of them are collinear.

If three of the four points are collinear, the number of lines is 4.
The answer is then $1 + 6 + 4 = 11$.

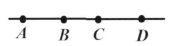

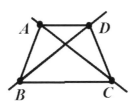

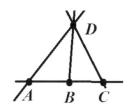

Example 1: How many angles in the figure are less than 180°?

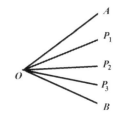

Solution:

Two lines form one angle. The question is to choose 2 lines among 5.

$\binom{5}{2} = 10$ angles.

> **The number of angles can be formed with *n* lines sharing one vertex is $\binom{n}{2}$.**

Example 2: How many angles in the figure are less than 180°?

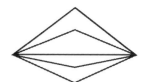

Solution:

We divide the figure into three sections:

For sections A and B, we each get $\binom{5}{2} = 10$ angles.

For section C, we count 4 angles less than 180.
The answer is $10 + 10 + 4 = 24$ angles.

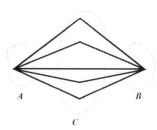

Example 3: Find angle $\angle AOB$ if the sum of all angles in the figure below is 180°. $\angle 1 = \angle 2 = \angle 3$.

Solution: 54°.

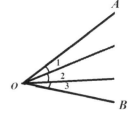

Two lines form one angle. The question is to choose 2 lines among 4.

$\binom{4}{2} = 6$ angles ($\angle 1, \angle 2, \angle 3; \angle 12, \angle 23, \angle 123$).

When we calculate the angles, we count $\angle 1$ and $\angle 3$ each three times and $\angle 2$ four times. So we have $3\angle 1 + 4\angle 2 + 3\angle 3 = 10 \angle 1 = 180°$. Thus $\angle 1 = 18°$ and $\angle AOB = 54°$.

> **Every two lines form 2 pairs of vertical angles when they intersect.**

> **If n lines intersect at one point, the number of vertical angles formed is**
>
> $$2 \times \binom{n}{2} = n(n-1).$$

Example 4: (1999 Mathcounts State Sprint) How many pairs of vertical angles are formed by five distinct lines that have a common point of intersection?

Solution: 20.

Method 1:
By the formula: $a_n = n(n-1)$ $\Rightarrow$ $a_5 = 5 \times 4 = 20$.

Method 2:
Figure (a) shows 2 pairs of vertical angles: (1, 3) and (2, 4).
Figure (b) shows 6 pairs of vertical angles:
(1, 4), (2, 5), (3, 6), (1-2, 4-5), (2-3, 5-6), (3-4, 6-1).
Figure (c) shows 12 pairs of vertical angles:
(1, 5), (2, 6), (3, 7), (4, 8),
(1-2, 5-6), (2-3, 6-7), (3-4, 7-8), (4-5, 8-1),
(1-2-3, 5-6-7), (2-3-4, 6-7-8), (3-4-5, 7-8-1), (4-5-6, 8-1-2).
Figure (c) shows 20 pairs of vertical angles:
(1, 6), (2, 7), (3, 8), (4, 9), (5, 10),
(1-2, 6-7), (2-3, 7-8), (3-4, 8-9), (4-5, 9-10), (5-6, 10-1),
(1-2-3, 6-7-8), (2-3-4, 7-8-9), (3-4-5, 8-9-10), (4-5-6, 9-10-1), (5-6-7, 10-1-2),
(1-2-3-4, 6-7-8-9), (2-3-4-5, 7-8-9-10), (3-4-5-6, 8-9-10-1), (4-5-6-7, 9-10-1-2), (5-6-7-8, 10-1-2-3).

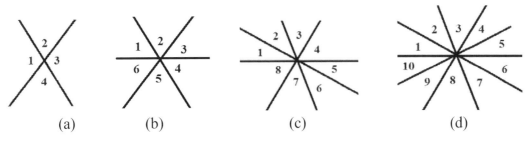

(a)   (b)   (c)   (d)

PROBLEMS

Problem 1: How many angles in the figure are less than 180°?

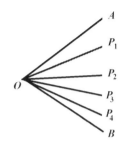

Problem 2: How many angles in the figure are less than 180°?

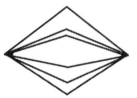

Problem 3: Find angle $\angle AOB$ if the sum of all angles in the figure below is 180°. $\angle 1 = \angle 2 = \angle 3 = \angle 4$.

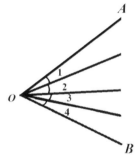

Problem 4: How many pairs of vertical angles are formed by 10 distinct lines that have a common point of intersection?

SOLUTIONS:

Problem 1: Solution:

Two lines form one angle. The question is to choose 2 lines among 6.

$$\binom{6}{2} = 15 \text{ angles.}$$

Problem 2: Solution:

We divide the figure into three sections:

For sections A and B, we each get $\binom{6}{2} = 15$ angles.

For section C, we count $3 \times 2 = 6$ angles less than 180.
The answer is $15 + 15 + 6 = 36$ angles.

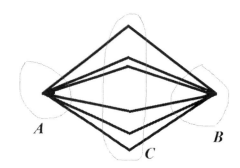

Problem 3: Solution: 54°.

Two lines form one angle. The question is to choose 2 lines among 5. $\binom{5}{2} = 10$ angles.

($\angle 1$, $\angle 2$, $\angle 3$, $\angle 4$; $\angle 12$, $\angle 23$, $\angle 34$; $\angle 123$, $\angle 234$; $\angle 1234$).

When we calculate the angles, we count $\angle 1$ and $\angle 4$ each four times, $\angle 2$ and $\angle 3$ each six times, and four times. So we have $4\angle 1 + 4\angle 4 + 6\angle 3 + 6\angle 2 = 20\angle 1 = 180°$. Thus $\angle 1 = 9°$ and $\angle AOB = 36°$.

Problem 4: Solution:

$$N = 2 \times \binom{n}{2} = 2 \times \binom{10}{2} = 90.$$

113

Example 1: (2003 Mathcounts Handbook) Seven points are distributed around a circle. All possible chords, using the given seven oints as endpoints, are drawn. What is the greatest possible number of points of intersection inside the circle? The point I is an example of one such point.

Solution:

The intersection points are determined by 4 points on the circle. The chords of a group of 4 points intersect only at one point. Then one intersection point corresponds to 4 points on the circle.
The greatest possible number of points of intersection inside the circle is

$$\binom{7}{4} = 35.$$

Theorem 1: The greatest number of intersection points of n lines on a plane is $\binom{n}{2}$.

The intersection points are determined by 2 lines. Two lines will intersect at one point.

Theorem 2: The greatest number of intersection points of all diagonals of a convex n-gon is $\binom{n}{4}$.

The intersection points are determined by 4 vertices on the circle. The diagonals of a group of 4 vertices intersect only at one point.

Theorem 3: The greatest number of intersection points of all possible chords drawn from n points on a circle is $\binom{n}{4}$.

The intersection points are determined by 4 points on the circle. The chords of a group of 4 points intersect only at one point. Then one intersection point corresponds to 4 points on the circle.

Example 2: (Mathcounts) What is the maximum of points of intersection when 5 lines intersect each other?

Solution: 10 (points).

Two lines will intersect at one point. The greatest number of intersection points of n lines on a plane is $\binom{n}{2} = \binom{5}{2} = 10$.

Example 3: (Mathcounts) What is maximum number of intersection points in a diagram with two circles of unequal diameter and a straight line?

Solution: 6 (points)

We get six points:

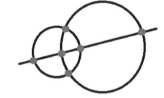

Example 4: (Mathcounts Handbooks) Three distinct lines in a plane may intersect in k points. What are all possible values of k?

Solution: 0, 1, 2, and 3

If three lines are parallel, they intersect at 0 point.

If two of the three lines are parallel, they intersect at 2 points.

If three lines are concurrent (they pass through one point), they intersect at 1 point.

If no three of the five lines are concurrent, they intersect at $\binom{3}{2} = 3$ points.

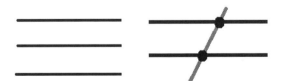 

Thepossible values are 0, 1, 2, and 3.

Example 5: As shown in the figure, line a is parallel to line b. There are 10 points on line a and nine points on line b. If we connect each point on a with each point on b, we get many lines. If no three of these line intersects at one point, what is the number of intersection points bertween a and b?

Solution:

We get one intersection point by connecting two points on a with two points on b.

We have $\binom{10}{2}$ ways to select two points from 10

points on a, and $\binom{9}{2}$ ways to select two points from 9

points on b.

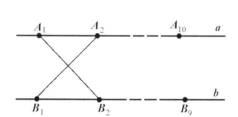

So the number of intersection points is

$\binom{10}{2} \times \binom{9}{2} = 45 \times 36 = 1620.$

PROBLEMS

Problem 1: What is the maximum number of intersection points inside a circle possible by all the chords formed by connecting six points on the circle?

Problem 2: (Mathcounts) What is the maximum number of intersection points possible for ten non-collinear lines in the same plane?

Problem 3: (Mathcounts) What is the largest number of points of intersection of a square, a circle and a line?

Problem 4: (Mathcounts Competitions) Five straight lines may lie in a plane in many different ways. For example, they may all intersect at a single point. Thus, one is a possitble number of intersection points for the five lines. Find the sum of all the whole numbers from 0 to 10 which cannot represent the total number of intersections of five distinct co-planar lines.

Problem 5: If all the diaonals of a regular hexagon are drawn, what is the greatest possible number of points of intersection inside the hexagon?

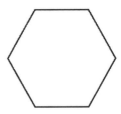

Problem 6: (2009 Mathcounts Handbook) Connect each point labeled on line *AD* with each point labeled on line *EH*. What is the total number of points of intersection between lines *AD* and *EH* that are created by the newly drawn segments? (Note: No three segments intersect at one point between the lines *AD* and *EH*.)

SOLUTIONS

Problem 1: Solution: 15.

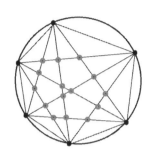

Method 1:
We count and we get 15 points.

Method 2:
The greatest number of intersection points of all possible chords

drawn from n points on a circle is $\binom{n}{4} = \binom{6}{4} = 15$.

Problem 2: Solution: 45.
Two lines will intersect at one point. The greatest number of intersection points of n lines

on a plane is $\binom{n}{2} = \binom{10}{2} = 45$.

Problem 3: Solution: 12.
One circle and one square can intersect at most 8 points. When one
line is joined, it can intersect two points with the circle and two
points with the square. Total we get $8 + 2 + 2 = 12$ points.

Problem 4: Solution: 5.
If five lines are parallel, they intersect at 0 point.
If four of the five lines are parallel, they intersect at 4 points.
If three of the five lines are parallel, and other two lines are parallel, they intersect at 6 points.
If three of the five lines are parallel, and other two lines are not parallel, they intersect at 7 points.

If five lines are concurrent (they pass through one point), they intersect at 1 point.

If four of the five lines are concurrent, they intersect at $\binom{5}{2} - \binom{4}{2} + 1 = 5$ points.

If three of the five lines are concurrent, they intersect at $\binom{5}{2} - \binom{3}{2} + 1 = 8$ points.

If no three of the five lines are concurrent, they intersect at $\binom{5}{2} = 10$ points.

The numbers of intersetion points not achieveable are 2 and 3. The sum of them is 5.

Problem 5: Solution: 13.
Method 1:
We draw and count. We get 13 points.

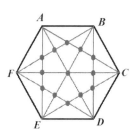

Method 2:
The intersection points are determined by 4 vertices on the circle. The diagonals of a group of 4 vertices intersect only at one point.
The greatest number of intersection points of all diagonals of a convex

n-gon is $\binom{n}{4} = \binom{6}{4} = 15$.

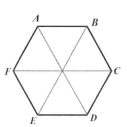

However, Four points of $AB - DE$, $BC - EF$, and $AC - DF$ will produce only one point of intersection.
So the answer is $15 - 3 + 1 = 13$.

Problem 6: Solution: 36.
 We get one intersection point by connecting two points on the top line with two points

on the bottom line. We have $\binom{4}{2}$ ways to select two points from $A, B, C, D,$ and $\binom{4}{2}$

ways to select two points from E, F, G, H.

So the number of intersection points is $\binom{4}{2} \times \binom{4}{2} = 6 \times 6 = 36$.

Example 1: (Mathcounts Competitions) How many triangles are in this figure?

Solution: 20.

Step 1: Count by 1.
We count the number of triangles formed by only one part.
We have 1 + 5 + 5 + 1 = 12.

Step 2: Count by 4.
We count the number of triangles formed by four parts.
Each red dot will have one triangle. We have 6 such dots and then we have 6 such triangles.

Step 2: Count by 9.
We count the number of triangles formed by nine parts. We have two.
Total we have 12 + 6 + 2 = 20 triangles.

Example 2: (Mathcounts Competitions) How many triangles can be traced using the segments in this diagram?

Solution: 12 triangles.

Step 1: Count by 1.
We count the number of triangles formed by only one part.

We have 6 such triangles.

Step 2: Count by 2.
We count the number of triangles formed by two parts.
We have 2 such triangles.

Step 3: Count by 3.
We count the number of triangles formed by
3 parts. Each red dot will have one triangle. We have two such triangles.
Total we have 6 + 2 + 4 = 12 triangles.

Example 3: (Mathcounts Competitions) Six distinct segments are drawn from one vertex of a triangle to the opposite side. What is the total number of triangles contained in the resulting figure?

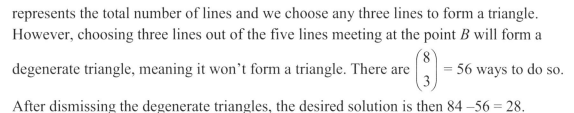

Solution: 28.

The total number of triangles possibly formed is $\binom{9}{3} = 84$, where 9

represents the total number of lines and we choose any three lines to form a triangle. However, choosing three lines out of the five lines meeting at the point B will form a degenerate triangle, meaning it won't form a triangle. There are $\binom{8}{3} = 56$ ways to do so.

After dismissing the degenerate triangles, the desired solution is then $84 - 56 = 28$.

Example 4: How many triangles are there?

Solution: 18.

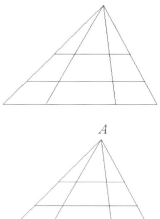

The total number of triangles possibly formed is $\binom{7}{3}$, where the

number 7 represents the total number of lines.

(1) Choosing three lines out of the four lines meeting at the point

A won't form a triangle; there are $\binom{4}{3}$ ways to do this.

(2) Any shape that has two parallel lines (out of a total three parallel lines) and one other line won't form a triangle. There are $\binom{3}{2} \times \binom{4}{1}$ ways to do this.

(3) Three parallel lines will not form a triangle as well. There are $\binom{3}{3}$ ways to choose

three parallel lines.

The desired solution is: $\binom{7}{3} - \binom{4}{3} - \binom{3}{2} \times \binom{4}{1} - \binom{3}{3} = 35 - 4 - 12 - 1 = 18.$

PROBLEMS

Problem 1: (Mathcounts Competitions) How many different triangles are in the picture?

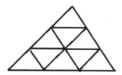

Problem 2: (Mathcounts Competitions) How many triangles are there in the figure shown?

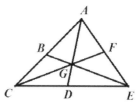

Problem 3: (Mathcounts Competitions) How many triangles are there in the figure?

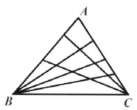

Problem 4: How many triangles are there?

Problem 5: (2000 Mathcounts State) How many triangles are in this figure?

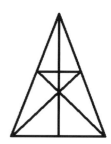

SOLUTIONS

Problem 1: Solution: 13.

Step 1: Count by 1.

We count the number of triangles formed by only one part. We have $1 + 3 + 5 = 9$.

Step 2: Count by 4.

We count the number of triangles formed by four parts.

Each red dot will have one triangle. We have 3 such dots and then we have 3 such triangles.

Step 3: Count by 9.

We count the number of triangles formed by nine parts. We have one.

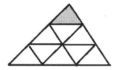 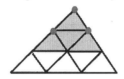 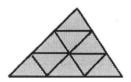

Total we have $9 + 3 + 1 = 13$ triangles.

Problem 2: Solution: 18.

Step 1: Count by 1.

We count the number of triangles formed by only one part.

We have $4 + 4 = 8$.

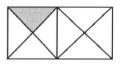

Step 2: Count by 2.

We count the number of triangles formed by two parts.

Each red dot will have one triangle. We have 4 such dots in one rectangle. So we have $4 \times 2 = 8$ such triangles.

Step 3: Count by 4.

We count the number of triangles formed by 4 parts. Each red dot will have one triangle. We have two such triangles.

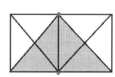

Total we have $8 + 8 + 2 = 18$ triangles.

Problem 3: Solution: 16.

The total number of triangles possibly formed is $\binom{6}{3} = 20$, where 6 represents the total

number of lines and we choose any three lines to form a triangle.

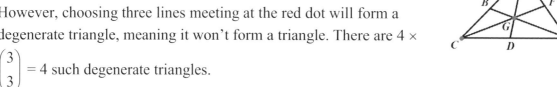

However, choosing three lines meeting at the red dot will form a
degenerate triangle, meaning it won't form a triangle. There are $4 \times$
$\binom{3}{3} = 4$ such degenerate triangles.

The desired solution is then $20 = 4 = 16$.

Problem 4: Solution: 42.

The total number of triangles possibly formed is $\binom{8}{3} = 56$, where 8 represents the total

number of lines and we choose any three lines to form a triangle.

However, choosing three lines out of the five lines meeting at the point B will form a

degenerate triangle, meaning it won't form a triangle. There are $\binom{5}{3}$ ways to do so.

Similarly, choosing three lines out of the four lines meeting at the point C will also not

form a triangle. There are $\binom{4}{3}$ ways to do so.

After dismissing the degenerate triangles, the desired solution is then

$$\binom{8}{3} - \binom{5}{3} - \binom{4}{3} = 56 - 10 - 4 = 42.$$

Problem 5: Solution: 24.
Method 1:
We count the triangles consisting of one triangle only and we get 8 triangles.

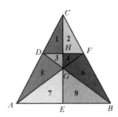

We count the triangles consisting of 2 triangles and we get 5 triangles:

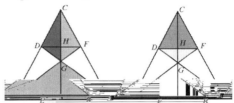

We count the triangles consisting of 3 triangles and we get 6 triangles:

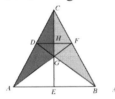 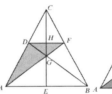 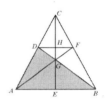

We count the triangles consisting of 4 triangles and we get 2 triangles:

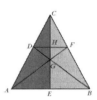

We count the triangles consisting of 5 triangles and we get 2 triangles:

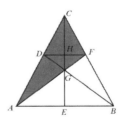 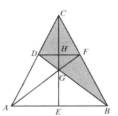

There are no triangles consisting of 6 or 7 triangles.

We count the triangles consisting of 8 triangles) and we get 1 triangle:

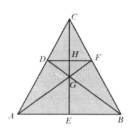

Total number of triangles: $8 + 5 + 6 + 2 + 2 + 1 = 24$.

Method 2:

There are 7 line segments in the given figure. Since three line segments can form one triangle, the total number of possible triangles that can be formed by 7 line segments is $\binom{7}{3} = 35$.

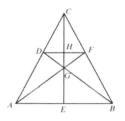

Choosing the three lines out of the three lines that intersect at the point D (as well as at F, G, A, B, and C) will not form a triangle. There are $6 \times \binom{3}{3} = 6$ ways to do this.

Two parallel lines and one other line will also not form a triangle. There are $\binom{2}{2} \times \binom{5}{1} = 5$ ways to do this. We must subtract the ways that do not form a triangle from the number of possible ways.

The desired solution is $35 - 6 - 5 = 24$.

Example 1: (Mathcounts Competitions) How many isosceles triangles can be created on this 2×4 geoboard?

Solution: 16 triangles.

We connect dots with lines:

Count by 1: we focus on one small square first. We see that each small square will be able to generate 4 isosceles triangles: $4 \times 3 = 12$.

Count by 2: we focus on two small squares then. We see that each red dot will be able to generate one isosceles triangle. We have $2 \times 2 = 4$ such isosceles triangles.

Total we get $12 + 4 = 16$ isosceles triangles.

Example 2: (Mathcounts Handbooks) Calculate the probability that three points chosen at random from the ten equally-spaced points shown form an equilateral triangle. Express your answer as a common fraction.

Solution: 1/8.

Step 1:

First we connect dots with lines.

Count by 1: We count the number of equilateral triangles formed by one part:

We get $1 + 3 + 5 = 9$.

Count by 4: We count the number of equilateral triangles formed by 4 parts:

Each red dot will produce an equilateral triangle. We get 3.

Count by 9: We count the number of equilateral triangles formed by 9 parts. We get 1 equilateral triangle.

We get total $9 + 3 + 1 = 13$ equilateral triangles.

Step 2:

We count irregular shapes.

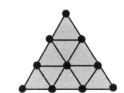

Each red dot will produce one equilateral triangle. We have 2 equilateral triangles.

We get total 13 + 2 = 15 equilateral triangles.

We have $\binom{10}{3} = 120$ triangles.

So the probability is $15/120 = 1/8$.

Example 3: (Mathcounts Competitions) Use the 6 points on the circle for vertices, how many triangles are possible that have point P as one vertex?

Solution: 10 triangles.

Method 1:
We know that every three points determine a triangle. Since we must have P as one of the three vertices, we only need to select two points from the rest of 5 points.

The answer is then $\binom{1}{1}\binom{5}{2} = 10$.

Method 2:
We know that every three points determine a triangle. Total number of possible triangles is $\binom{6}{3} = 20$. The number of triangles that can be formed without P is $\binom{5}{3} = 10$.

The answer is then $\binom{6}{3} - \binom{5}{3} = 10$.

Theorem:
The maximum number of triangles can be formed by using these n points in the plane as vertices is $N = \binom{n}{3}$.

Example 4: Given that a 3×7 rectangular array of dots, how many triangles can be formed whose vertices are dots in the array?

Solution: 1200.

There are $\binom{12}{3}$ sets of 3 points. We must exclude from our count those sets of three points that are collinear.

There are 3 horizontal lines with seven points each. These 3 lines contain $3\binom{7}{3}$ sets of 3 collinear points.

Similarly, there are $7\binom{3}{3} + 5\binom{3}{3} + 5\binom{3}{3} + 3\binom{3}{3} + 3\binom{3}{3} + 2\binom{3}{3}$ sets of 3 collinear points.

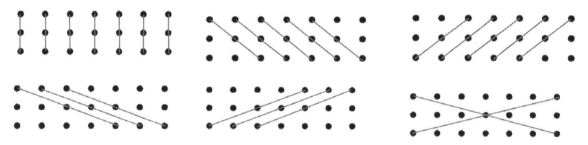

The number of triangles is then $\binom{21}{3} - 3\binom{7}{3} - 25\binom{3}{3} = 1330 - 105 - 25 = 1200$.

PROBLEMS

Problem 1: (Mathcounts Handbooks) How many different sized isosceles triangles can be formed by joining three or more dots on the grid of dots which are equally spaced vertically and horizontally?

```
•  •  •  •
•  •  •  •
•  •  •  •
•  •  •  •
```

Problem 2: (Mathcounts) What is the probability that three points randomly selected from the nine equally-spaced points shown form an isosceles triangle? Express your answer as a common fraction.

```
•  •  •
•  •  •
•  •  •
```

Problem 3: Each point in the hexagonal lattice is one unit from its nearest neighbor. How many triangles can be formed by joining three points?

```
   •   •
 •   •   •
   •   •
```

Problem 4: Twelve lattice points are arranged along the edges of a 3 × 3 rectangle as shown. How many triangles have all three of their vertices among these points?

```
•    •    •    •

•    •    •    •

•    •    •    •
```

Problem 5: How many triangles can be formed by connecting three points of the figure?

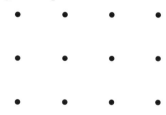

130

SOLUTIONS:

Problem 1: Solution: 11.
We count

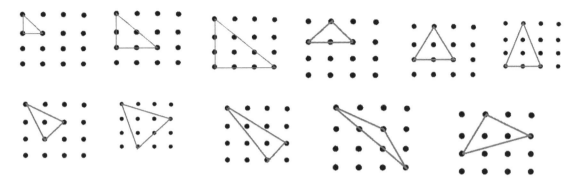

Problem 2: Solution: 3/7.
Case I: Each small square will generate 4 isosceles triangles. We
have $4 \times 4 = 16$ isosceles triangles.

Case II: We get 4 isosceles triangles:

Case III: each red dot will generate one isosceles triangle. We get 4 isosceles triangles.

Case IV: each red dot will generate one isosceles triangle. We get $4 \times 2 = 8$ isosceles
triangles.

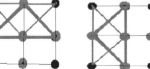

Case V: each red dot will generate one isosceles triangle. We get 4 isosceles triangles.

We get total $16 + 4 + 4 + 8 + 4 =$ 36 equilateral triangles.

We have $\binom{9}{3} = 84$ triangles.

So the probability is $36/84 = 3/7$.

Problem 3: Solution:

The greatest number of triangles that can be formed is $\binom{7}{3} = 35$.

Three points on the same red line shown cannot form a triangle.
So the solution is $35 - 3 = 32$.

Problem 4: Solution: 200.

There are $\binom{12}{3}$ sets of 3 points. We must exclude from our count those sets of three

points that are collinear. There are 3 horizontal lines with four points each. These 3 lines

contain $3\binom{4}{3}$ sets of 3 collinear points. Similarly, there are $4\binom{3}{3} + 4\binom{3}{3}$ sets of 3

collinear points that determine lines of slope ± 1. Because there are no other sets of 3
collinear points, the number of triangles is the total sets minus the degenerate triangles

equals $\binom{12}{3} - 3\binom{4}{3} - 8\binom{3}{3} = 200$.

Problem 5: Solution: 25.
Method 1:
$$\binom{5}{2}\binom{2}{1} + \binom{5}{1}\binom{2}{2} = 20 + 5 = 25$$
Method 2:
$$\binom{7}{3} - \binom{5}{3} = 35 - 10 = 25.$$

Example 1: (Mathcounts) How many different rectangles are in the figure?

Solution: 9 (rectangles)

Method 1:
Count by 1: We get $1 \times 4 = 4$ rectangles.

Count by 2: We get $2 \times 2 = 4$ rectangles.

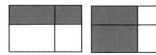

Count by 4: We get 1 rectangle.
The answer is $4 + 4 + 1 = 9$.

Method 2:
We have $\binom{3}{2}$ ways to select the two vertical sides and $\binom{3}{2}$ ways to select the two horizontal sides of a rectangle.

The answer is $\binom{3}{2} \times \binom{3}{2} = 9$.

Counting rectangles

For a rectangle with h horizontal lines and v vertical lines, the total number of rectangles that can be counted is $N = \binom{h}{2} \times \binom{v}{2}$.

Example 2: (Mathcounts Handbook) How many squares are there in the three-by-three grid of squares?

Solution: 14.

Method 1:
Count by 1: We get 1 × 9 = 9 squares.

Count by 4: We get 2 × 2 = 4 squares.

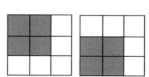

Count by 9: We get 1 square.
The answer is 9 + 4 + 1 = 14.

Method 2:
We have $3^2 + 2^2 + 1^2 = 14$ squares.

Counting squares in a rectangle with *m* rows and *n* columns

Case I: $m \neq n$. N, the number of squares in a $m \times n$ rectangular grid with $m \geq n$ is

$$N = m \times n + (m - 1) \times (n - 1) + (m - 2) \times (n - 2) + \ldots + (m - I) \times 1$$

where I is $m - n$.

Example 3: (Mathcounts) A brick mantel over a fireplace consists of rectangles as shown. What is the total number of rectangles in the pattern?

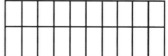

Solution: 165.

We have $\binom{11}{2}$ ways to select the two vertical sides and $\binom{3}{2}$ ways to select the two horizontal sides of a rectangle.

The answer is $\binom{11}{2} \times \binom{3}{2} = 165$.

Example 4: (Mathcounts) How many squares are contained in the figure shown?

Solution: 55 (squares).

We have $5^2 + 4^2 + 3^2 + 2^2 + 1^2 = 55$ squares.

Example 5: Consider the 3×4 figure shown in the right. How many 1×2 rectangles are there?

Solution:

Method 1:
$1 \times 3 \times 3 = 9$.

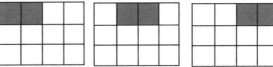

$1 \times 4 \times 2 = 8$.

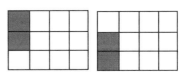

Total we get $9 + 8 = 17$.

Method 2:
$N = m \times (n-1) + n(m-1) = 3 \times (4-1) + 4(3-1) = 17$.

How many 1×2 rectangles are there?	$N = m \times (n-1) + n(m-1)$
How many $1 \times l$ rectangles are there?	$N = m \times (n-(l-1)) + n(m-(l-1))$
How many $s \times l$ rectangles are there?	

$$N = [m-(l-1)] \times [(n-(s-1)] + [n-(l-1)] \times [m-(s-1)]$$

Example 6: (Mathcounts) How many squares are pictured?

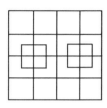

Solution: 40 (squares)

The total number of squares of counted from the 4 by 4 square equals $4^2 + 3^2 + 2^2 + 1^2 = 16 + 9 + 4 + 1 = 30$.

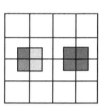

We count $5 \times 2 = 10$ more.
Total 40.

Example 7: The 4×6 rectangular grid of squares shown below contains a shaded square. What is the probability that a randomly selected rectangular sub-region contains the shaded area?

Solution: 2/7.

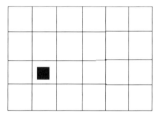

The total number of rectangles equals $\binom{7}{2} \times \binom{5}{2} = 210$.

The number of rectangular sub-regions that contain the shaded area is

$$\binom{2}{1} \times \binom{5}{1} \times \binom{3}{1} \times \binom{2}{1} = 60$$

The probability equals 60/210= 2/7.

PROBLEMS

Problem 1: (Mathcounts) All angles are right angles. How many rectangles are in this diagram?

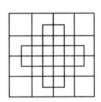

Problem 2: (Mathcounts) The figure shown is constructed of 16 congruent squares. What is the probability that a randomly selected rectangle within the figure is a square? Express your answer as a common fraction.

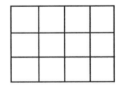

Problem 3: (1999 Mathcounts National) How many squares are pictured?

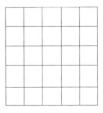

Problem 4: Consider the 3×4 figure shown in the right. How many 1×3 rectangles are there?

Problem 5: A 5×5 square is shown below. How many 1×2 rectangles are there?

Problem 6: How many squares are there?

Problem 7: (2003 Mathcounts Chapter) An 8 by 8 checkerboard has alternating black and white squares. How many distinct squares, with sides on the grid lines of the checkerboard (horizontal and vertical) and containing at least 4 black squares, can be drawn on the checkerboard?

SOLUTIONS

Problem 1: Solution:

The total number of rectangles equals $\binom{4}{2} \times \binom{4}{2} = 36$.

Problem 2: Solution:

The total number of rectangles equals $\binom{5}{2} \times \binom{5}{2} = 100$.

The total number of squares equals $4^2 + 3^2 + 2^2 + 1^2 = 16 + 9 + 4 + 1 = 30$.
The probability is $30/100 = 3/10$.

Problem 3: Solution:
The number of squares of counted from the 4 by 4 square equals
$4^2 + 3^2 + 2^2 + 1^2 = 16 + 9 + 4 + 1 = 30$.

The number of squares generated by following 1 by 1 squares is
$1 \times 4 \times 5 = 20$.

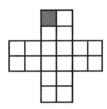

The number of squares generated by following 2 by 2 squares is
$5 + 4 = 9$.

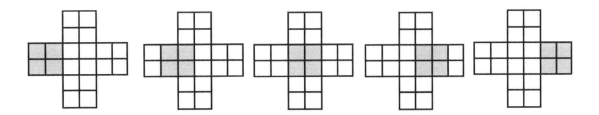

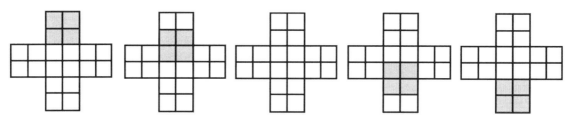

We see 4 more squares:

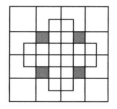

And 4 squares

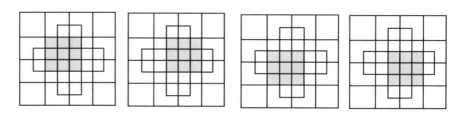

The total number of squares is 30 + 20 + 9 + 4 + 4 = 67.

Problem 4: Solution:

$$N = m \times (n - (l-1)) + n(m - (l-1)) = 3 \times (4 - (3-1)) + 4(3 - (3-1)) = 10$$

Problem 5: Solution: 40.

Method 1:

(1) $N = m \times (n-1) + n(m-1) = 5 \times (5-1) + 5(5-1) = 40$.

Method 2:

The length of a 5×5 square is 5 units. The square contains 4 line segments of length two and 5 line segments of length one. The total number of 1×2 squares is $4 \times 5 \times 2 = 40$.

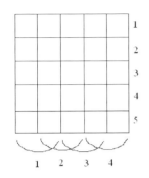 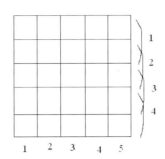

Problem 6: Solution: 20.

We have $m = 4$ and $n = 3$, so the total number of squares is:

$N = 4 \times 3 + 3 \times 2 + 2 \times 1 = 20$.

Problem 7:

Solution: 91.

$6^2 + 5^2 + 4^2 + 3^2 + 2^2 + 1^1 = 91$.

Example 1: (Mathcounts) What is the probability that four randomly selected points on the geoboard shown will be vertices of a square? Express your answer as a common fraction.

Solution: $\dfrac{1}{21}$.

Method 1:

There are $\dbinom{9}{4} = 126$ ways to select four points.

There are 4 + 1 + 1 = 6 squares:

The probability is 6/126 = 1/21.

Method 2:

There are $\dbinom{9}{4} = 126$ ways to select four points.

There are $\dfrac{n^2(n^2-1)}{12} = \dfrac{3^2(3^2-1)}{12} = 6$ ways that these four points are the vertices of a square.

The probability is 6/126 = 1/21.

The number of squares formed by a $n \times n$ arrays of dots:

Method 1: If we have a $n \times n$ array of points, where n is the number of dots in any row or column, and we want to find out how many squares have all four vertices from the array, we can use this formula: $N = \dfrac{n^2(n^2-1)}{12}$.

Method 2: If we have a $n \times n$ array of points, where n is the number of dots in any row or column, and we want to find out how many squares have all four vertices from the array, we can use this formula:
$N = 1 \times (n-1)^2 + 2 \times (n-2)^2 + 3 \times (n-3)^2 + 4 \times (n-4)^2 + \dots + (n-1) \times 1^2$.

Method 3: If we have an $n \times n$ array of points, and we want to find out how many squares have all four vertices from the array,

(1). Count the number of squares formed by only vertical and horizontal lines.

That is: $N_1 = (n-1)^2 + (n-2)^2 + ... + 1^2$.

(2). Count the number of squares that are formed by non-vertical/horizontal lines (which is the same as the number of non-inclined squares calculated by using $(n-1)(n-1)$ array of points).

That is: $N_2 = (n-2)^2 + (n-3)^2 ... + 1^2$

(3). Continue the process until the end $N = N_1 + N_2 + ... + 1^2$.

Example 2: (Mathcounts) What is the probability that four different points chosen at random from the fifteen equally-spaced points shown are the vertices of a square? Express your answer as a common fraction.

Solution: $\dfrac{2}{195}$.

The number of squares $= \dfrac{3(3^2-1)(2 \times 5-3)}{12} = 14$

The probability is $P = \dfrac{14}{\binom{15}{4}} = \dfrac{14}{1365} = \dfrac{2}{195}$.

The number of squares formed by a $m \times n$ $(m \le n)$ arrays of dots:

$\dfrac{m(m^2-1)(2n-m)}{12}$.

Example 3: How many different sized squares are there?

Solution: 5.

Method 1: We count directly and we get 5 of them.

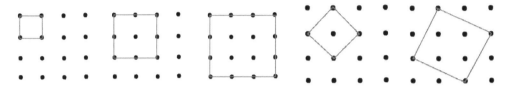

Method 2:

n is the number of the dots in a row for a $n \times n$ array.

There are $N = \left\lfloor \dfrac{(n-1)(n+3)}{4} \right\rfloor = \left\lfloor \dfrac{(4-1)(4+3)}{4} \right\rfloor = 5$ different sized square for a 4 by 4

array.

Method 3:

For a $n \times n$ array of points, the number of squares with different sizes is the same as the number of all squares in a $(n-1) \times (n-1)$ array of points.

$N = 1 \times [(4-1)-1]^2 + 2 \times [(4-1)-2]^2 = 4 + 1 = 5.$

The number of different sized squares in a $n \times n$ array is $N = \left\lfloor \dfrac{(n-1)(n+3)}{4} \right\rfloor$, where n

is the number of the dots in a row for a $n \times n$ array.

PROBLEMS

Problem 1: 2006 Mathcounts Handbook) How many squares with horizontal and vertical sides can be formed using points of the grid as vertices?

Problem 2: How many squares can be drawn from the 4 × 4 array of points with the vertices on the points?

Problem 3: (1993 Mathcounts National Target) Find the probability that four randomly selected points on the geoboard below will be the vertices of a square? Express your answer as a common fraction.

Problem 4: (Mathcounts) The dots on the rectangular grid are equally spaced horizontally and vertically. How many rectangles have all their vertices among the dots of the 3 × 4 grid?

Problem 5: (2004 Mathcounts Handbook) On this 5 by 5 grid of dots, one square is shown in the diagram. Including this square, how many different sizes of squares can be formed using four dots of this array as vertices?

SOLUTIONS

Problem 1: Solution: 14.
This problem is the same as to calculate how many squares in the figure: We get $3^2 + 2^2 + 1^2 = 14$.

Problem 2: Solution: 20.
Method 1:

By the formula we have $\Rightarrow N = \dfrac{4^2(4^2-1)}{12} = 20$ squares.

Method 2:

(1) Count the number of squares formed by only vertical and horizontal lines.
$$N_1 = (4-1)^2 + (4-2)^2 + 1^2 = 9 + 4 + 1 = 14$$

(2) Count the number of squares that are formed by non-vertical/horizontal lines. This is the same as the number of non-inclined squares calculated by using $(n-1)(n-1)$ array of points. $N_2 = (4-2)^2 + 1^2 = 5$.

(3). Continue the process until the end: $N_3 = (4-3)^2 = 1$

(4). $N = N_1 + N_2 + N_3 = 14 + 5 + 1 = 20$

Method 3:
$$N = 1 \times (n-1)^2 + 2 \times (n-2)^2 + 3 \times (n-3)^2 + 4 \times (n-4)^2 + \dots + (n-1) \times 1^2$$

$$= 1 \times (4-1)^2 + 2 \times (4-2)^2 + 3 \times (4-3)^2 = 1 \times 3^2 + 2 \times 2^2 + 3 \times 1^1 = 9 + 8 + 3 = 20.$$

Problem 3: Solution: $\dfrac{1}{91}$.

There are $\dbinom{16}{4} = 1820$ ways to select four points.

There are $N = \dfrac{4^2(4^2-1)}{12} = 20$ ways that these four points are the vertices of a square.

The probability is $20/1820 = \dfrac{1}{91}$.

Problem 4: Solution: 20 (rectangles).

We count the number of rectangles in the figure below:

We get $\begin{pmatrix} 4 \\ 2 \end{pmatrix} \times \begin{pmatrix} 3 \\ 2 \end{pmatrix} = 18$ rectangles.

We count two more inclined squares:

Total we get 20 rectangles.

Problem 5: Solution: 8.

Method 1:

We count 8 of them.

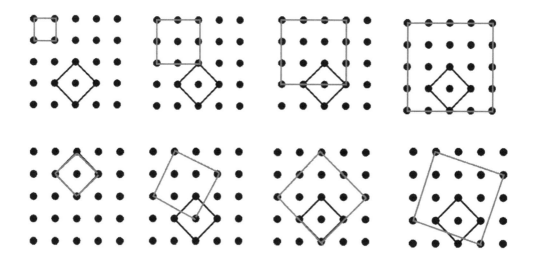

Method 2:

$$N = \left\lfloor \frac{(n-1)(n+3)}{4} \right\rfloor = \left\lfloor \frac{(5-1)(5+3)}{4} \right\rfloor = \frac{32}{4} = 8.$$

Example 1: (2001 Mathcounts State Sprint) Sixty-four cubes are placed together to create a larger cube. How many cubes with integer dimensions are in the $4 \times 4 \times 4$ cube?

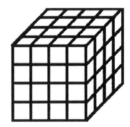

Solution: 100.

There are $4 \times 4 \times 4 + 3 \times 3 \times 3 + 2 \times 2 \times 2 + 1 \times 1 \times 1 = 100$ many cubes with integer dimensions are in the $4 \times 4 \times 4$ cube.

Counting Cubes

The formula for the total number of cubes, N, in a given large rectangular solid with dimension $m \times n \times r$ is

$N = m \times n \times r + (m-1) \times (n-1) \times (r-1) + (m-2) \times (n-2) \times (r-2) + \ldots + (m - I) \times (r - J) \times 1$. ($I$ and J are integers).

Example 2: Sixty-four cubes are placed together to create a larger cube. How many rectangular prisms with integer dimensions are in the $4 \times 4 \times 4$ cube?

Solution: 3375.

$$N = \binom{m+1}{2} \times \binom{n+1}{2} \times \binom{r+1}{2} = \binom{4+1}{2} \times \binom{4+1}{2} \times \binom{4+1}{2}$$
$$= 1000.$$

Counting Rectangular Prisms

The total number of rectangular solids, N, in a given large rectangular solid with

dimension $m \times n \times r$ is $N = \binom{m+1}{2} \times \binom{n+1}{2} \times \binom{r+1}{2}$.

Example 3: A big solid of $8 \times 10 \times 11$ is made up of 880 small cubes. How many $1 \times 1 \times 2$ small rectangular prisms are there?

Solution: 2362.

Method 1: (Direct counting)

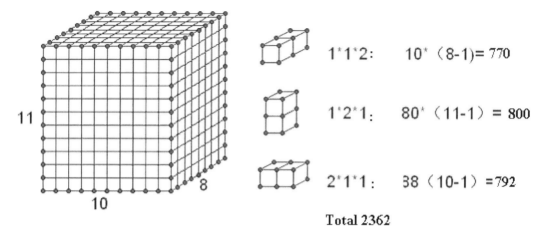

1^*1^*2: $10^* (8-1) = 770$

1^*2^*1: $80^* (11-1) = 800$

2^*1^*1: $88 (10-1) = 792$

Total 2362

Method 2: By using the formula,
$m \times n \times (r-1) + m \times (n-1) \times r + (m-1) \times n \times r$, we get the answer 2362.

Counting $1 \times 1 \times 2$ small rectangular prisms

The number of $1 \times 1 \times 2$ small rectangular prisms:
$m \times n \times (r-1) + m \times (n-1) \times r + (m-1) \times n \times r$

Counting $1 \times 1 \times 3$ small rectangular prisms

The number of $1 \times 1 \times 3$ small rectangular prisms:
$m \times n \times (r-2) + m \times (n-2) \times r + (m-2) \times n \times r$

Example 4: (Mathcounts) How many cubes 3cm on each edge will it take to fill a rectangular box 9cm × 6cm × 6cm?

Solution: 12 (cubes)

The number of cubes is $\dfrac{9}{3} \times \dfrac{6}{3} \times \dfrac{6}{3} = 12$.

Example 5: (Mathcounts) What is the maximum number of rectangular blocks with dimensions 3 inches by 5 inches by 2 inches that will fit into a box 15 inches by 30 inches by 12 inches?

Solution: 180 (blocks).

The number of cubes is $\dfrac{30}{5} \times \dfrac{15}{3} \times \dfrac{12}{2} = 180$.

Example 6: (2007 Mathcounts Handbook)) A 4 × 4 × 4 inch cube originally built from 1 × 1 × 1 inch cubes is cut into exactly 29 cubes with integer edge lengths and no material left over. How many of the 29 cubes are 2 × 2 × 2 inch cubes?

Solution: 5.

The 29 cubes are in the forms of 3 × 3 × 3, 2 × 2 × 2 , or 1 × 1 × 1.
Let x, y, and z be the number of cubes 3 × 3 × 3, 2 × 2 × 2 , or 1 × 1 × 1, respectively.
We have
$27x + 8y + z = 64$ (1)
$x + y + z = 29$ (2)
$(1) - (2)$: $26x + 7y = 35$ (3)
We write (3) as $y = 5 - \dfrac{26x}{7} = 5 - \dfrac{2 \times 13 \times x}{7}$.

Since y is integer, x must be either 0 or 7 (ignored). So $x = 0$ and $y = 5$.

PROBLEMS

Problem 1: (Mathcounts) What is the total number of cubes of any size with integral side lengths in the $5 \times 5 \times 5$ cube shown?

Problem 2: Find the total number of rectangular solids, N, given the large rectangular solid with dimension $10 \times 8 \times 11$ in the figure below.

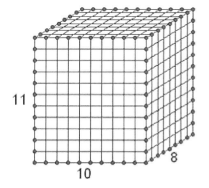

Problem 3: Find the total number of cubes, N, given a large rectangular solid with dimension $10 \times 8 \times 11$.

Problem 4: A big solid of $8 \times 10 \times 11$ is made up of 880 small cubes. How many $1 \times 1 \times 3$ small rectangular prisms are there?

Problem 5: (2004 Canadian Math Competition)A large block, which has dimensions n by 11 by 10, is made up of a number of unit cubes and one 2 by 1 by 1 block. There are exactly 2362 positions in which the 2 by 1 by 1 block can be placed. What is the value of n?

Problem 6: (Mathcounts Competitions) A rectangular block of dimensions 24 by 30 by 36 is cut into 3 by 3 by 3 cubes. How many such cubes are formed?

Problem 7: (Mathcounts Competitions) What is the maximum number of cubes measuring 5 cm on an edge that can be obtained by cutting a solid cube that measures 1 m on an edge?

SOLUTIONS

Problem 1: Solution: 225.

There are $5 \times 5 \times 5 + 4 \times 4 \times 4 + 3 \times 3 \times 3 + 2 \times 2 \times 2 + 1 \times 1 \times 1 = 225$ cubes with integer dimensions are in the $5 \times 5 \times 5$ cube.

Problem 2: Solution: 130,680.

There are $N = \binom{m+1}{2} \times \binom{n+1}{2} \times \binom{r+1}{2} =$

$\binom{10+1}{2} \times \binom{8+1}{2} \times \binom{11+1}{2} = 55 \times 36 \times 66 = 130,680$ rectangular solids in the solid.

Problem 3: Solution: 2532.

The number of total cubes in the solid equals
$m \times n \times r + (m-1) \times (n-1) \times (r-1) + (m-2) \times (n-2) \times (r-2) + \ldots + (m-I) \times (r-J)$
$\times 1 = 10 \times 8 \times 11 + (10-1) \times (8-1) \times (11-1) + (10-2) \times (8-2) \times (11-2) + \ldots + (10-7) \times (8-7) \times (11-7) = 2532$.

Problem 4: Solution: 2362.

By using the formula, $m \times n \times (r-2) + m \times (n-2) \times r + (m-2) \times n \times r$
$= 8 \times 10 \times (11-2) + 8 \times (10-2) \times 11 + (8-2) \times 10 \times 11 = 2084$.

Problem 5: Solution: 8.

The number of $1 \times 1 \times 2$ small rectangular prisms:
$m \times n \times (r-1) + m \times (n-1) \times r + (m-1) \times n \times r = 2362$.
$10 \times n \times (11-1) + 10 \times (n-1) \times 11 + (10-1) \times n \times 11 = 2362$.
$100n + 110n - 110 + 99n = 2362$. $n = 8$.

Problem 6: Solution: 960 (cubes).

The number of cubes is $\frac{24}{3} \times \frac{30}{3} \times \frac{36}{3} = 8 \times 10 \times 12 = 960$.

Problem 7: Solution: 8000. The number of cubes is $\frac{100}{5} \times \frac{100}{5} \times \frac{100}{5} = 8000$.

Example 1: (Mathcounts) What is the maximum number of non-overlapping regions created by four distinct lines in a plane?

Solution: 11 (regions).

Method 1:
We count directly:

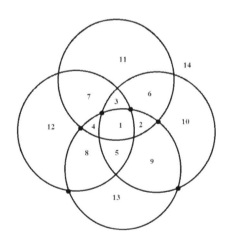

Method 2:

$$\binom{n}{0}+\binom{n}{1}+\binom{n}{2}=\frac{n(n+1)}{2}+1=\frac{4(4+1)}{2}+1=11$$

> Maximum number of regions n lines can divide a plane is N and
> $$N=\binom{n}{0}+\binom{n}{1}+\binom{n}{2}=\frac{n(n+1)}{2}+1.$$

Example 2: At most how many parts can 4 circles cut a plane?

Solution: 22.

Method 1: One circle can at most cut the plane into 2 parts.
 2 circles can at most cut the plane into 4 parts.
 3 circles at most can cut the plane into 8 parts.
4 circles will cut the plane into 14 parts.

Method 2: Using the formula:

$$N=2[\binom{n}{2}+1]=n^2-n+2=5^2-5+2=22 \ .$$

> Maximum number of regions n circles can divide a plane is N and
> $$N=2[\binom{n}{2}+1]=n^2-n+2.$$

154

Example 3: What is the maximum number of parts can 2 triangles cut a plane?

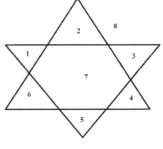

Solution: 62.
Method 1:
We count directly and we get 7 parts.

Method 2:
Five triangles cut the plane into N regions and

Five triangles cut the plane into N regions and

$$N = 2\binom{n-1}{0} + 6\binom{n-1}{1} + 6\binom{n-1}{2} = 2 + 3n(n-1) = 2 + 3 \times 2 \times (2-1) = 8.$$

> Maximum number of regions n triangles can divide a plane is N and
> $$N = 2\binom{n-1}{0} + 6\binom{n-1}{1} + 6\binom{n-1}{2} = 2 + 3n(n-1).$$

Example 4: What is the maximum number of parts can 2 rectangles cut a plane?

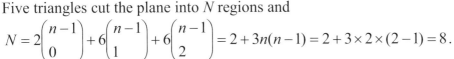

Solution: 10.

Method 1:
We count directly and we get 10 parts.

Method 2:
Five triangles cut the plane into N regions and

$$N = 2\binom{n-1}{0} + 8\binom{n-1}{1} + 8\binom{n-1}{2} = 2 + 4n(n-1) = 2 + 4 \times 2 \times (2-1) = 10.$$

> Maximum number of regions n rectangles can divide a plane is N and
> $$N = 2\binom{n-1}{0} + 8\binom{n-1}{1} + 8\binom{n-1}{2} = 2 + 4n(n-1)$$

> Maximum number of regions n convex m-gons can divide a plane is $N = mn(n-1) + 2$.

> Maximum number of regions formed by n points on a circle when chords are constructed in the circle by jointing n points is N and $N = \binom{n}{4} + \binom{n}{2} + 1$.

> Maximum number of regions formed by diagonals of a convex polygon:
> $$N = 1 + \binom{n}{2} - n + \binom{n}{4}.$$

Example 5: Find the maximum number of regions formed by joining 3 planes in the space.

Solution:

Method 1:
One plane divides the space into $1 + 1 = 2$ regions.
We add the second plane. The intersection of this plane and the first plane is a line. The intersection line will divide the second plane into two parts. The intersection line will also divide the first plane into two parts. The increase of the parts is then $1 + 1 = 2$. The number of regions is then $1 + 1 + 2 = 4$.
We add the third plane. The third plane will intersect the first two planes at two lines. These two lines will cut the third plane into three parts (increase two parts) and increase two parts for the first two planes.
The number of regions is then $1 + 1 + 2 + 4 = 8$.

Method 2:
$$N = \frac{n^3}{6} + \frac{5}{6}n + 1 = \frac{3^3}{6} + \frac{5 \times 3}{6} + 1 = 8.$$

> Maximum number of regions n lines can divide a plane is N and
> $$N = \binom{n}{0} + \binom{n}{1} + \binom{n}{2} + \binom{n}{3} = \frac{n^3}{6} + \frac{5}{6}n + 1.$$

PROBLEMS

Problem 1: (Mathcounts) What is the maximum number of regions in the plane created by three distinct lines, no two of which are parallel?

Problem 2: What is the greatest number of regions can be formed by 5 circles in a plane?

Problem 3: One rectangle can cut the plane into 2 parts. What is the maximum number of parts can three rectangles can cut the plane? What is the maximum number of parts can five rectangles can cut the plane?

Problem 4: What is the maximum number of parts can 5 triangles cut a plane?

Problem 5: There are 10 lines in a plane. Four of the lines are parallel. At most how many regions the plane can be divided by these lines?

Problem 6: Find the maximum number of regions formed by joining 7 points on the circle.

Problem 7: Find the maximum number of regions formed by joining n planes in the space.

SOLUTIONS:

Problem 1: Solution: 7 (regions).
Method 1: We draw the figure and count. We get 7.

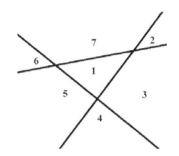

Method 2: $\binom{n}{0}+\binom{n}{1}+\binom{n}{2}=\binom{3}{0}+\binom{3}{1}+\binom{3}{2}=1+3+3=7$.

Problem 2: Solution: 22 parts..
Method 1: One circle can at most cut the plane into 2 parts.
2 circles can at most cut the plane into 4 parts.
3 circles at most can cut the plane into 8 parts.
These three numbers can be derived by simply drawing.

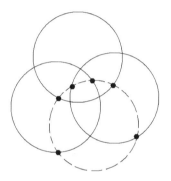

Now we insert the 4th circle, which is tougher to just eye and count
the number of regions. In order to cut as many parts as possible, the
4th circle must have 2 intersection points with each of the 3 circles.
Then we get 6 intersection points. These 6 points cut the 4th circle
into 6 arcs, each arc cuts the part it is in into 2 parts, i.e. each arc add 1 part to the number
of parts we got before, so 6 arcs will add 6 parts and we then know that 4 circles will cut
the plane into 8 + 6 =14 parts. Similarly, we know that 5 circles will cut the plane into 14
+ 8 = 22 parts.

Method 2: $N=2\binom{n-1}{0}+2\binom{n-1}{1}+2\binom{n-1}{2}=n^2-n+2=5^2-5+2=22$.

Problem 3: Solution: 82.
Method 1:
One rectangle will cut the plane into 2 regions; 2 rectangles will cut the plane into 10
regions; 3 rectangles will cut the plane into 26
regions.

Method 2:
By the formula, we have:

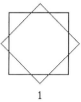
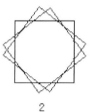

1   2

$$N = 2\binom{n-1}{0} + 8\binom{n-1}{1} + 8\binom{n-1}{2} = 2 + 4n(n-1) = 2 + 4 \times 3 \times (3-1) = 26.$$

Problem 4: Solution: 62.

Five triangles cut the plane into N regions and

$$N = 2\binom{n-1}{0} + 6\binom{n-1}{1} + 6\binom{n-1}{2} = 2 + 3n(n-1) = 2 + 3 \times 5(5-1) = 62.$$

Problem 5: Solution: 50.

6 non-parallel lines can at most divide the plane into $2 + 2 + 3 + 4 + 5 + 6 = 22$ regions. If we add one line from the four parallel lines, this line at most has 6 intersecting points with the 6 lines. This line is divided into 7 sections. Each section cuts the region it is in into two parts. So these are 7 more regions. Similarly we know that adding one line will increase 7 regions. So the answer is $22 + 7 \times 4 = 50$ regions.

Problem 6: Solution: 57.

The maximum number of regions formed by joining 7 points on the circle is

$$N = \binom{n}{4} + \binom{n}{2} + 1 = \binom{7}{4} + \binom{7}{2} + 1 = 57.$$

Problem 7: Solution:

One plane divides the space into $1 + 1 = 2$ regions.

We add the second plane. The intersection of this plane and the first plane is a line. The intersection line will divide the second plane into two parts. The intersection line will also divide the first plane into two parts. The increase of the parts is then $1 + 1 = 2$. The number of regions is then $1 + 1 + 2 = 4$.

We add the third plane. The third plane will intersect the first two planes at two lines. These two lines will cut the third plane into three parts (increase two parts) and increase two parts for the first two planes.

The number of regions is then $1 + 1 + 2 + 4 = 8$.

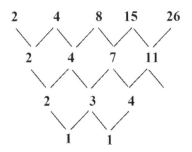

We add fourth plane and the space is divided into 15 parts.

We add fifth plane and the space is divided into 26 parts.

By the Newton's Little Formula,

$$a_n = A\binom{n-1}{0} + B\binom{n-1}{1} + C\binom{n-1}{2} + \cdots + K\binom{n-1}{m}$$

$$= 2\binom{n-1}{0} + 2\binom{n-1}{1} + 2\binom{n-1}{2} + \binom{n-1}{3}$$

$$= 2 + 2n - 2 + 2\frac{(n-1)(n-2)}{2} + \frac{(n-1)(n-2)(n-3)}{6}$$

$$= 2n + (n-1)(n-2) + \frac{(n-1)(n-2)(n-3)}{6} = \frac{n^3}{6} + \frac{5}{6}n + 1.$$

Example 1: (Mathcounts) What is the greatest number of pieces into which a circular pizza can be cut using five straight edge-to-edge cuts?

Solution: 16 (pieces)

Method 1: We cut the circle directly and count. We are able to get 16 pieces.

Method 2:

We know that the maximum number of regions n lines can divide a plane is N and $N = \binom{n}{0} + \binom{n}{1} + \binom{n}{2} = \frac{n(n+1)}{2} + 1$.

So 5 lines can cut the plane into $\frac{5(5+1)}{2} + 1 = 16$ parts.

Now we add one circle.

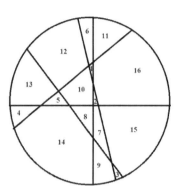

This circle can enclose all the 16 parts inside it. Therefore, 5 lines at most can cut 1 circle into 16 parts.

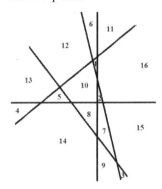
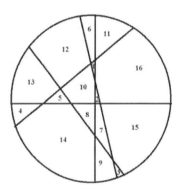

Example 2: (1990 Mathcounts National) In a plane, four distinct lines intersect the interior of a circle forming regions within the circle. If m represents the maximum number of regions that can be formed and n represents the minimum number, find $m + n$.

Solution: 16.

Step 1: Since we want to get the maximum number of regions, we cut the circle in such a way that no line will go through the same point. There are $m = 11$ regions, as shown in the left figure.

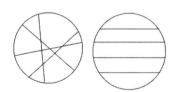

Step 2: In order to obtain the minimum number of regions, we cut the circle in such a way so that no lines intersect. There are $n = 5$ regions, as shown in the right figure. $m + n = 16$.

> Maximum number of points of intersection by n circles and m lines is N and
> $$N = 2\binom{n}{2} + \binom{m}{2} + 2mn = n(n-1) + \frac{m(m-1)}{2} + 2mn$$

> Maximum number of regions n circles and m lines can divide a plane is N and
> $$N = 2\binom{n}{2} + \binom{m}{2} + 2mn + m + 1 = n(n-1) + \frac{m(m-1)}{2} + 2mn + m + 1$$

Example 3: Five circles and 1 line can at most cut a plane into how many parts?

Solution: 32.

Method 1:
We know that 5 circles can cut the plane into 22 parts. Now we add one more line. Since one line can at most have 2 intersection points with a circle, one line can at most have 10 intersection points with 5 circles.

These 10 points divide this line into 11 sections; 9 of them are inside the circles and 2 of them are outside the circles.

Each of the 9 line sections inside the circles cuts the part it is in into 2 parts, i.e. each line section adds one more region. 9 line sections add 9 regions.

Two line sections outside the circles cuts the plane into 2 regions, so these two line sections add only one more region. So these 11 line sections totally add 10 regions. The desired answer will then be: $22 + 10 = 32$ regions.

Method 2:
$$N = n(n-1) + \frac{m(m-1)}{2} + 2mn + m + 1 = 5(5-1) + \frac{1(1-1)}{2} + 2 \times 5 + 1 + 1 = 32.$$

Example 4: Two circles and three straight lines lie in the same plane. If neither the circles nor the lines are coincident, what is the maximum possible number of regions that can be formed?

Solution: 21.

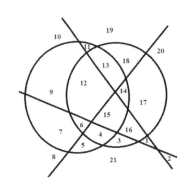

Method 1: We draw the figure and count and we get 21 regions.

Method 2:
$$N = n(n-1) + \frac{m(m-1)}{2} + 2mn + m + 1$$
$$= 2(2-1) + \frac{3(3-1)}{2} + 2 \times 2 \times 3 + 3 + 1 = 21.$$

Example 5: There are 1 point on the sides AB, 3 points on the sides BC, and 2 points on side CA of triangle ABC as shown in the figure. Connect each vertex with the points on the opposite side. How many parts the triangle ABC is cut into if no three of these connecting lines are collinear?

Solution: 18.

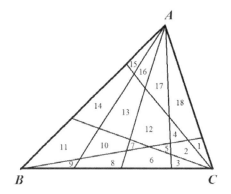

Method 1: We draw the figure and we count up to 18 parts.

Method 2:
$$N = lm + mn + nl + l + m + n + 1$$
$$= 1 \times 2 + 2 \times 3 + 3 \times 1 + 1 + 2 + 3 + 1 = 18.$$

Example 6: Find the maximum number of regions formed by joining 5 chords in sphere.

Solution:

It is the same as the maximum number of regions formed by joining 5 planes in space: N
$$= \binom{n}{0} + \binom{n}{1} + \binom{n}{2} + \binom{n}{3} = \frac{n^3}{6} + \frac{5}{6}n + 1 = \frac{5^3}{6} + \frac{5}{6} \times 5 = 26.$$

PROBLEMS

Problem 1: (Mathcounts) What is the smallest number of line segments that can be drawn within a circle to separate it into 11 distinct regions?

Problem 2: One circle and 5 lines can at most cut a plane into how many parts?

Problem 3: (2002 Mathcounts National) Two circles and a square lie in the plane. What is the maximum number of points of intersection of two or more of these three figures?

Problem 4: (1999 Mathcounts National) Two circles and three straight lines lie in the same plane. If neither the circles nor the lines are coincident, what is the maximum possible number of points of intersection?

Problem 5: There are n points on the sides AB, l points on the sides BC, and m points on side CA of triangle ABC. Connect each vertex with the points on the opposite side. How many parts the triangle ABC is cut into if no three of these connecting lines are collinear?

Problem 6: (2007 Mathcounts Handbook) Three segments can divide a circular region into at most seven regions. What is the maximum number of regions that a circular region can be divided into by 100 segments?

SOLUTIONS

Problem 1: Solution: 4.
Method 1: We cut the circle directly and count. We are able to use 4 cuts.

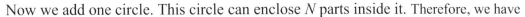

Method 2:
We know that the maximum number of regions n lines can divide a plane is
N and $N = \binom{n}{0} + \binom{n}{1} + \binom{n}{2} = \frac{n(n+1)}{2} + 1$.

Now we add one circle. This circle can enclose N parts inside it. Therefore, we have

$\frac{n(n+1)}{2} + 1 = 11 \qquad \Rightarrow \qquad n(n+1) = 20$.

Solving for n and we get $n = 4$ or $n = -5$ (ignored).

Problem 2: Solution: 26.
We know that 5 lines can cut the plane into 16 parts. Now we add one circle. This circle can at most have 2 intersection points with each line, so it can at most have 10 intersection points. Theses 10 points divide the circle into 10 arcs. Each arc cuts the part that the arc is in into 2 parts. In other words, each arc adds one more part. So 10 arcs add 10 more regions. Therefore, 1 circle and 5 lines at most can cut a plane into $16 + 10 = 26$ parts.

Method 2: $N = n(n-1) + \frac{m(m-1)}{2} + 2mn + m + 1 = 1(1-1) + \frac{5(5-1)}{2} + 2 \times 5 + 5 + 1 = 26$.

Problem 3: Solution: 18.
Two intersecting circles have 2 intersection points. One square has 8 intersection points with a circle and 16 intersection points with two circles. So there are a total of $2 + 16 = 18$ points of intersection.

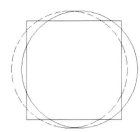

Problem 4: Solution: 17.
Method 1: Three lines will have 3 points of intersection. One circle will have at most 2 points of intersection with each line. Each circle will add 6 more points and 2 circles will add 12 points of intersection with the lines.
However, two circles will have at most 2 points of intersection with themselves. This will add 2 points of intersection. The total points of intersection are $3 + 12 + 2 = 17$.

Method 2: The number of intersection points is N and

$$N = n(n-1) + \frac{m(m-1)}{2} + 2mn + m + 1 = 2(2-1) + 3(3-1)/2 + 2 \times 2 \times 3 = 17.$$

Problem 5: Solution: $N = lm + mn + nl + l + m + n + 1$.

We draw l lines from vertex A to its opposite site and we get $l + 1$ regions.

Now we draw one line from vertex B. This line is cut into $l + 1$ sections by l lines we drew from vertex A. So the number of regions will be increased by $l + 1$. Since we draw m lines from B, the number of regions will be increased by $m(l + 1)$.

Last we draw one line from C. This line is cut into $l + m + 1$ sections by the $m + 1$ lines. Since we draw n lines from C, the number of regions will be increased by $n(l + m + 1)$.

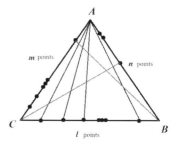

Therefore the number of regions of triangle ABC is

$l + 1 + m(l + 1) + n(l + m + 1)$

$= lm + mn + nl + l + m + n + 1$.

Problem 6: Solution: 5051.

Method 1:

We know that the maximum number of regions 100 lines can divide a plane is N and $N =$

$$\binom{n}{0} + \binom{n}{1} + \binom{n}{2} = \frac{n(n+1)}{2} + 1 = \frac{100(100+1)}{2} + 1 = 5051.$$

Now we add one circle. This circle can enclose N parts inside it. Therefore, the answer is 5051.

Method 2:

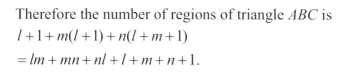

By <u>Newton's Little Formula for n^{th} term</u>:

$$a_n = 2\binom{n-1}{0} + 2\binom{n-1}{1} + \binom{n-1}{2} = \frac{n(n+1)}{2} + 1 \text{ and } a_{100} = \frac{100(100+1)}{2} + 1 = 5051.$$

Example 1: (1996 Mathcounts Chapter) When all possible diagonals from one vertex of a 50- sided convex polygon, how many triangles are formed?

Solution: 48 triangles.

We draw a few figures as shown.
We see that the number of triangles
formed by drawing all possible diagonals
from one vertex of a convex n-gon is $n - 2$.
So $n - 2 = 50 - 2 = 48$ triangles.

Example 2: There are 10 points inside a triangle. They are connected by non-intersecting segments with each other and with the vertices of the triangle in such a way that the triangle is dissected into triangles. How many smaller triangles do we have?

Solution: 21.

Method 1:
$n-1$ points can divide the triangle into a_{n-1} smaller triangles.
When we add one more point P_n, if P_n is
inside one of the smaller triangles, as in
figure (a), the vertex of the original
triangle and P_n will cut the smaller
triangle into three triangles, that is, two
more triangles will be produced.
If P_n is on the common side of two
smaller triangles, as shown in figure (b),
the vertices of these two triangles and P_n

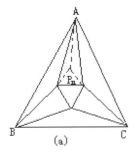
(a)

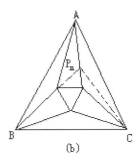
(b)

will cut the two smaller triangles into four, that is, the number of triangles is increased by 2. So n points inside the triangle will cut the triangle into the number of triangles:

$a_n = a_{n-1} + 2$.

$a_0 = 1$, $a_1 = a_0 + 2$, $a_2 = a_1 + 2$,   ..., $a_n = a_{n-1} + 2$.
Adding them together, we get $a_n = 2n + 1$.
So $N = 2n + 1 = 2 \times 10 + 1 = 21$.

Method 2:

We know that the sum of three interior angles of a triangle is $180°$. One point inside the square will produce a $360°$ angle. N points will produce the angle of $N \times 360°$. The measure of all angles will be this angle plus the original angle of the triangle: $N \times 360° + 180°$.

When this is divided by $180°$, it will give the number of triangles that can be formed.

$$\frac{N \times 360 + 180}{180} = \frac{10 \times 360 + 180}{180} = 21.$$

Example 3: There are 10 points inside a square. They are connected by non-intersecting segments with each other and with the vertices of the square in such a way that the square is dissected into triangles. How many triangles do we have?

Solution: 22.

Method 1:
One point inside the square will form 4 triangles. Two points will produce 6 triangles; 3 points will produce 8 triangles. By this pattern we see that the formula is $2n + 2 = 2 \times 10 + 2 = 22$

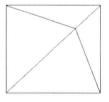 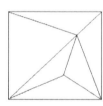

Method 2:
We know that the sum of three interior angles of a triangle is $180°$.
One point inside the square will produce a $360°$ angle, so N points will produce the angle of $N \times 360°$.
This angle in addition to the original angle of the square becomes $N \times 360° + 360°$.

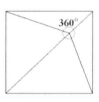

Since the sum of three interior angles of one triangle is $180°$, then the total number of triangles that are formed is: $\dfrac{N \times 360 + 360}{180} = \dfrac{10 \times 360 + 360}{180} = 22.$

Example 4: Select 6 points on the circumference of a circle. Select 4 points inside the circle. Connect these points to form non-overlapping triangles. What is the greatest number of triangles can be formed?

Solution: 12.

Any given 6 points can form 4 non-overlapping triangles as shown in Figure 1. In Figure 2, using point A we can produce one non-overlapping triangle; using point B we can produce two more non-overlapping triangles. So if we select one point inside each of the four triangles in Figure 1, we will get a total of 12 non-overlapping triangles.

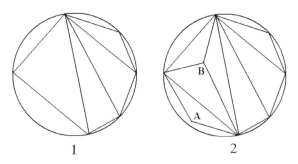

1   2

PROBLEMS

Problem 1: There are 20 points inside a triangle. They are connected by non-intersecting segments with each other and with the vertices of the triangle in such a way that the triangle is dissected into triangles. How many smaller triangles do we have?

Problem 2: There are 20 points inside a square. They are connected by non-intersecting segments with each other and with the vertices of the square in such a way that the square is dissected into triangles. How many triangles do we have?

Problem 3: Select 8 points on the circumference of a circle. Select 4 points inside the circle. Connect these points to form non-overlapping triangles. What is the greatest number of triangles can be formed?

SOLUTIONS

Problem 1: Solution: 41.

Method 1: By using the formula: $N = 2n + 1 = 2 \times 20 + 1 = 41$.

Method 2: $n-1$ points can divide the triangle into a_{n-1} smaller triangles.

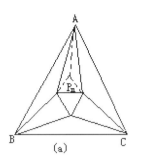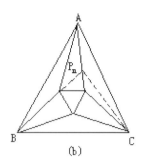

When we add one more point P_n, if P_n is inside one of the smaller triangles, as in figure (a), the vertex of the original triangle and P_n will cut the smaller triangle into three triangles, that is, two more triangles will be produced.

If P_n is on the common side of two smaller triangles, as shown in figure (b), the vertices of these two triangles and P_n will cut the two smaller triangles into four, that is, the number of triangles is increased by 2. So n points inside the triangle will cut the triangle into the number of triangles: $a_n = a_{n-1} + 2$.

$a_0 = 1$, $a_1 = a_0 + 2$, $a_2 = a_1 + 2$, ..., $a_n = a_{n-1} + 2$.
Adding them together, we get $a_n = 2n + 1$.

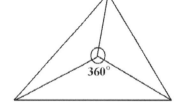

Method 3: We know that the sum of three interior angles of a triangle is 180°. One point inside the square will produce a 360° angle. N points will produce the angle of $N \times 360°$. The measure of all angles will be this angle plus the original angle of the triangle: $N \times 360° + 180°$.

When this is divided by 180°, it will give the number of triangles that can be formed.

$$\frac{N \times 360 + 180}{180} = \frac{20 \times 360 + 180}{180} = 41.$$

If we want to cut off these small triangles, we need to have $(20 \times 3 - 3)/2$ cuts. We multiply 20 by 3 because there are three sides in a triangle and we divide by 2 because every side is counted twice.

Problem 2: Solution: 42.

Method 1:
One point inside the square will form 4 triangles. Two points will produce 6 triangles; 3 points will produce 8 triangles. By this pattern we see that the formula is $2n + 2$.

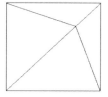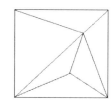

Thus, $N = 2n + 2 = 2 \times 20 + 2 = 42$

Method 2:
We know that the sum of three interior angles of a triangle is $180°$.

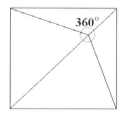

One point inside the square will produce a $360°$ angle, so N points will produce the angle of $N \times 360°$.

This angle in addition to the original angle of the square becomes $N \times 360° + 360°$.

Since the sum of three interior angles of one triangle is $180°$, then the total number of triangles that are formed is: $\dfrac{N \times 360 + 360}{180} = \dfrac{20 \times 360 + 360}{180} = 42$.

Problem 3: Solution: 18.
Any given 8 points can form 6 non-overlapping triangles as shown in Figure 1. In Figure 2, using point B we can produce two more non-overlapping triangles. So if we select one point inside each of the six triangles in Figure 1, we will get a total of $6 \times 3 = 18$ non-overlapping triangles.

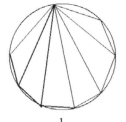

1   2

Example 1: (Mathcounts) Select four different digits from the set { 1, 2, 3, 4} and place one in each box. What is the largest possible product that can be obtained?

☐☐ × ☐☐

Solution: 1312.

The two largest digits, 3 and 4, are placed as the tens digit of the two 2-digt numbers. Then, 1 is the units digit of 41 and 2 is the units digit of 32. The greatest product is $\overline{41} \times \overline{32} = 1312$.

Note: $\overline{42} \times \overline{31} = 1302$, which is smaller than 1312. $\overline{ab}$ stands for a 2-digit number.

Example 2: Given 4 digits 1, 2, 3, and 4 to form two 2-digit numbers. What is the smallest possible product?

Solution:

The smallest product is $\overline{13} \times \overline{24} = 312$.

Note: $\overline{14} \times \overline{23} = 322$, which is larger than 312.

THEROEMS:

(1). If $a > b$ and $c > d$, where a, b, c, and d are digits, since
$$\overline{ad} \times \overline{bc} - \overline{ac} \times \overline{bd} = (10a + d)(10b + c) - (10a + c)(10b + d) = 10(a - b)(c - d) > 0,$$
then $\overline{ad} \times \overline{bc} > \overline{ac} \times \overline{bd}$.

(2) Given $a < b < c < d$, where a, b, c, and d are distinct digits. These digits are used to form a pair of two-digit integers where no digit can be used twice.

(2.1) The greatest product can be achieved by $\overline{da} \times \overline{cb}$.
First place the two largest digits (d and c) as the leading digits of the two 2-digit numbers; then select the remaining smallest digit (a, not b) and adjoin it to the largest digit (d). The digit b will then go with the digit c to form the second two-digit integer.

(2.2) The smallest product can be achieved by $\overline{ac} \times \overline{bd}$.

173

First place the two smallest digits (*a* and *b*) as the leading digits of the two 2-digit numbers; then select the smallest digit left (*c* in this case) to be attached with the smallest digit (the digit *a*). The digit *d* will then go with the digit *b*.

Example 3: (1995 Mathcounts State) What is the greatest possible product of a four-digit number and a three-digit number obtained from seven distinct digits?

Solution:

Put 9 and 8 this way:

9
8

Next we put the digits 7 and 6. 7 needs to be with 8 and 6 goes with 9 (let the difference of two resulting numbers be as close as possible). We see that the difference is $96 - 87 = 9$. which is indeed smaller than $97 - 86 = 11$.

9	6
8	7

then we put 5 going with 87 and 4 with 96 (let the difference of two resulting numbers be as close as possible).

9	6	4
8	7	5

Then we have 3 left. 3 needs to go with 875 (smaller number comparing with 964).

9	6	4	
8	7	5	3

The greatest possible product is then 8437892.

PROBLEMS

Problem 1: (Mathcounts) The digits 2, 4, 6 and 8 are placed in the following multiplication problem so that the resulting product is as large as possible. Which digit must be placed in the units place of the smaller factor? □□×□□

Problem 2: Fill each square with a digit of 4, 5, 6, 7, 8, and 9 such that the product is the greatest. □□□×□□□

Problem 3: Fill each square with a digit of 2, 3, 6, 8, and 9 in the box such that the product is the greatest. □□×□□□

Problem 4: (Mathcounts) The digits 0, 2, 4, 6, and 8 are to be placed one in each box, in the multiplication problem shown, so that the product is as large as possible. What is the product?

$$
\begin{array}{r}
\square\ \square\ \square \\
\times \qquad \square\ \square \\
\hline
\end{array}
$$

Problem 5: (Mathcounts) Using each of the digits 3, 4, 5, and 6 exactly once, find the two 2-digit numbers with the least possible product.

$$
\begin{array}{r}
\square\ \square \\
\times \quad \square\ \square \\
\hline
\end{array}
$$

Problem 6: (Mathcounts) What is the largest possible product obtained by placing the digits 5, 6, 7, 8, and 9 in the boxes shown?

$$
\begin{array}{r}
\square\ \square\ \square \\
\times \qquad \square\ \square \\
\hline
\end{array}
$$

SOLUTIONS

Problem 1: Solution: 5248.

Step 1: We put the two largest digits 8 and 6 in the leftmost boxes, the tens digit, first.

☐☐ : **8**
☐☐: **6**

Step 2: We select the digit 4 to be adjoined to 6 and the digit 2 to be adjoined to the digit 8 (the smaller digit goes with the larger number).

☐☐ : **82**
☐☐: **64**

The greatest product is $82 \times 64 = 5248$.

Problem 2: Solution: 843500.

Step 1: We put the largest digits 9 and 8 in the leftmost boxes first.
☐☐☐ : **9**
☐☐☐: **8**

Step 2: We select the digit 6 to be attached to 9 and the digit 7 to be attached to the digit 8 (the smaller digit goes with the larger number).
☐☐☐ : **96**
☐☐☐: **87**

Step 3: We select the digit 4 to be attached to 96 and the digit 5 to be attached to the digit 86 (the smaller digit goes with the larger number).
☐☐☐ : **964**
☐☐☐ : **875**
The greatest product is 843500.

Problem 3: Solution: 80166.

Step 1: Add one more box or "digit" and put the digits 9 and 8 in the leftmost boxes first.
□□□ : **9**
□□□: **8**

Step 2: We select the digit 6 to be attached to 9 and the digit 7 to be attached to the digit 8 (the smaller digit goes with the larger digit).
□□□ : **93**
□□□: **86**

Step 3: We have the digit 2 left and we imagine that we also have a digit 0. We attach 2 which is larger than 0 to the smaller number which is 86.
□□□ : **93**
□□□: **862**

The greatest product is: 93 × 862 = 80166.
Note: 932 × 86 = 80152, 96 × 832 = 79872, and 962 × 83 = 79846, but these are all smaller than our final answer.

Problem 4: Solution: 52480.
Step 1: We put the largest digits 8 and 6 in the leftmost boxes first.
□□□ : **8**
□□□: **6**

Step 2: We select the digit 4 to be attached to 6 and the digit 2 to be attached to the digit 7 (the smaller digit goes with the larger number).
□□□ : **82**
□□□: **64**

Step 3: We select the digit 0 to be attached to any of 82 or 64.
□□□ : **82**
□□□ : **640**
The greatest product is 52480.

Problem 5: Solution: 35 and 46.

Step 1: We put the two smallest digits 3 and 4 in the leftmost boxes, the tens digit, first.

□□ : **3**

□□: **4**

Step 2: We select the digit 5 to be adjoined to 3 and the digit 6 to be adjoined to the digit 4 (the smaller digit goes with the smaller number).

□□ : **35**

□□: **46**

The greatest product is $35 \times 46 = 1610$.

Problem 6: Solution: 84,000.

Step 1: We put the largest digits 9 and 8 in the leftmost boxes first.

□□□ : **9**

□□□: **8**

Step 2: We select the digit 7 to be attached to 8 and the digit 6 to be attached to the digit 9 (the smaller digit goes with the larger number).

□□□ : **96**

□□□: **87**

Step 3: We select the digit 5 to be attached to any of 87.

□□□ : **96**

□□□ : **875**

The greatest product is 84000.

Number Of Digits Used To Name Page Numbers

Pages 1 through 9 use	9×1	=	9	digits
Pages 10 through 99 use	90×2	=	180	digits
Pages 100 through 999 use	900×3	=	2700	digits
Pages 1000 through 9999 use	9000×4	=	36000	digits

Appearing Frequency Of Each Digit

Units digits:	1	out of	10
Ten's digit	10	out of	100
Hundred's digit	100	out of	1000
Thousand's digit	1000	out of	10000

Distribution Of Digits In Integers From 0 To 999

	0-99	100-199	200-299	300-399	400-499	500-599	600-699	700-799	800-899	900-999
0	10	20	20	20	20	20	20	20	20	20
1	20	120	20	20	20	20	20	20	20	20
2	20	20	120	20	20	20	20	20	20	20
3	20	20	20	120	20	20	20	20	20	20
4	20	20	20	20	120	20	20	20	20	20
5	20	20	20	20	20	120	20	20	20	20
6	20	20	20	20	20	20	120	20	20	20
7	20	20	20	20	20	20	20	120	20	20
8	20	20	20	20	20	20	20	20	120	20
9	20	20	20	20	20	20	20	20	20	120

For example, digit "1" appears 120 times when writing the numbers from 100 to 199. It appears 20 times when writing other numbers with the same hundreds digit, like numbers from 200 to 299, or 800 to 899.

179

Example 1: It takes 852 digits to number the pages of a book consecutively. How many pages are there in the book?

Solution:

Pages 1 through 9 use	9×1	$=$	9	digits
Pages 10 through 99 use	90×2	$=$	180	digits
Pages 100 through 999 use	900×3	$=$	2700	digits
Pages 1000 through 9999 use	9000×4	$=$	3600	digits

For a total of 189 digits for pages 1 through 99. That leaves 663 digits remaining to make the required total of 852 digits. These are obtained by going 221 pages beyond page 99, through page 320.

Example 2: A book has 500 pages numbered 1, 2, 3, 4, and so on. How many times does the digit 1 appear in the page numbers?

Solution:

Units place: the digit "1" appears once in every ten. Since 500 has 50 tens, the digit "1" will appear 50 times in units place.

Tens place: the digit "1" appears ten times in every hundred. Since 500 has 5 hundreds, the digit "1" will appear 50 times in tens place.

Hundred place: the digit "1" will appear 100 times in the hundreds place (100, 102,..., 199). The digit "1" will appear a total of 200 times in the page numbers.

Example 3. (1999 Mathcounts Chapter Target) The pages of a book are numbered consecutively, beginning with page 1. If 1020 digits are used to number the pages, how many pages are in the book?

Solution: 376.

Pages 1 through 9 use	9×1	$=$	9	digits
Pages 10 through 99 use	90×2	$=$	180	digits
Pages 100 through x use	$x \times 3$	$=$	$1020 - 180 - 9 = 831$	digits

$x = 277$. The number of pages $= 277 + 90 + 9 = 376$.

PROBLEMS

Problem 1: (1999 Mathcounts Chapter Sprint #30) Lockers are numbered with consecutive positive integers beginning with 1, and the digit 2 is used exactly 106 times. What is the number of the last locker?

Problem 2. (Mathcounts) Carlin wrote a 477-page book on the history of mathematics. She numbered the pages by hand, beginning with page 1. How many total digits did she write when numbering the pages?

Problem 3: (MMPC 2001 #11) To number all the pages of a book, the printer uses 651 digits. How many pages does the book have?

Problem 4: 510 digits were printed in numbering the pages of a book. If the first page of the book is numbered "1", how many pages does the book have?

Problem 5: (Mathcounts) A book contains 250 pages. How many times is the digit 2 used in numbering the pages?

Problem 6: (Mathcounts) If you use 999 digits to write page numbers consecutively starting with 1, how many page numbers could you write?

SOLUTIONS

Problem 1: Solution:
Since there are 40 twos from 1 to 199 and we are given that the digit 2 is used exactly 106 times, there should be 106 – 40 = 66 twos left starting from 200.
There are 10 twos from 200 to 209, 11 twos from 210 to 219, 22 twos from 220 to 229, 11 twos from 230 to 239, and 11 twos from 240 to 249.
This provides a total of 65 twos, so the last locker is one more from 249, or 250.

Problem 2. Solution: 1323.

Pages 1 through 9 use	9×1	=	9	digits
Pages 10 through 99 use	90×2	=	180	digits
Pages 100 through 477 use	$(477 - 100 + 1) \times 3$	=	1134	digits

The number of digits = 9 + 180 + 1134 = 1123.

Problem 3: Solution:
Let x be the number of pages. Clearly $100 < x < 999$. So the number of digits is $9 + 2 \times 90 + 3(x - 99) = 651$. Thus $x = 253$.
Or let y be the number of three-digit (hundred) pages. So the number of digits is $9 + 2 \times 90 + 3x = 651$. Thus $y = 154$. So the total pages will be $154 + 90 + 9 = 253$. 90 is the number of 2-digit pages and 9 is the number of one-digit page.

Problem 4: Solution:
Let x be the number of pages. Clearly $x < 500$. So the number of digits is $9 + 2 \times 90 + 3(x - 99) = 510$. Thus $x = 107$. The book has $9 + 90 + 107 = 206$.

Problem 5: Solution: 106 times.
The digit "2" appears 20 + 20 = 40 times when writing pages 1 through 199.
The digit "2" will appear 11 times when writing 200 – 209, 210 – 219. 230 – 239, and 240 – 249, appear 21 times when writing the number from 220 to 229, and one time for 250. So $11 \times 4 + 21 + 1 = 66$ times in writing pages 200 to 250. The sum of 40 + 66 = 106.

Problem 6: Solution: 369.
Let x be the number of pages. Clearly $x < 999$. So the number of digits is $9 + 2 \times 90 + 3(x - 99) = 999$. Thus $x = 270$. The book has $9 + 90 + 270 = 369$.

Example 1: (1999 Mathcounts Chapter Target) A cube is painted red and then cut into 1000 congruent cubes. How many of these cubes are painted red on at least two faces?

Solution: 300.

This is a $10 \times 10 \times 10$ cube.

There are 8 small cubes painted 3 faces and $(n-2) \times 2 \times 6 = (10-2) \times 2 \times 6 = 8 \times 2 \times 6 = 96$ cubes painted 2 faces.

Total $8 + 96 = 104$ cubes are painted red on at least two faces.

How many cubes painted how many faces?				
Cube dimension	4×4×4	5×5×5	$n \times n \times n$	$m \times n \times r$
3 sides painted	8	8	8	8
2 sides painted	24	36	$(n-2)^1 \times 2 \times 6$	$4(m-2) + 4(n-2) + 4(r-2)$
1 sides painted	24	54	$(n-2)^2 \times 1 \times 6$	$2(m-2)(n-2) + 2(m-2)(r-2) + 2(n-2)(r-2)$
0 sides painted	8	27	$(n-2)^3$	$(m-2)(n-2)(r-2)$
Total number of cubes	64	125	n^3	$m \times n \times r$

Example 2: (1988 NC Math League) The surface of a $10 \times 10 \times 10$ cube is painted purple. It is then cut into 1000 small cubes of equal size. How many of these small cubes will have an odd number of faces painted purple?

Solution: 392.

The number of cubes with three faces painted is 8 and the number of cubes with one face painted is $6(10-2)^2 = 384$. The number of small cubes with an odd number of faces painted purple is equal to the sum $384 + 8 = 392$.

Example 3: (1973 AMC) One thousand unit cubes are fastened together to form a large cube with edge length 10 units. This cube is painted and then separated into the original cubes. Find the number of these unit cubes which have at least one face painted.

Solution: 488.

The unpainted cubes form a $8 \times 8 \times 8$ cube of interior cubes. Therefore $10^3 - 8^3 = 488$ cubes will have at least one face painted.

PROBLEMS

Problem 1: (1994 Mathcounts National Sprint Round) The dimensions of a rectangular block are 30 cm, 16 cm, and 12 cm. It is made from cubes which are each 1 cm^3 in volume. If the outside of the block is painted red, what percent of the block is made up of cubes with exactly two sides painted red? Express your answer to the nearest tenth.

Problem 2: (2004 Mathcounts National Sprint) A rectangular block of candy 10 inches by 10 inches by 5 inches is coated on all faces with a very thin layer of chocolate. The block of candy is then cut into cubes measuring 1 inch by 1 inch by 1 inch. What percent of the cubes have no chocolate on them? Express your answer to the nearest tenth.

Problem 3: (1997 Mathcounts State Team) Unit cubes are glued together to make a cube several units on each sides. Some of the faces of the large cube are painted. When the cube is taken apart, there are exactly 45 unit cubes without any paint. How many unit cubes were used to create the larger cube?

Problem 4: 2006 (Mathcounts Handbook). A 2 by 3 by 4 rectangular prism is painted and then cut into 24 unit cubes. If a unit cube will be selected at random, what is the probability that it will have fewer than two painted faces? Express your answer as a common fraction

SOLUTIONS

Problem 1: Solution: 3.6%.

There are $4(m-2) + 4(n-2) + 4(r-2) = 208$ cubes with two-sides painted.

The percent of the block made up of cubes with exactly two sides painted red is

$$\frac{208}{30 \times 16 \times 12} = 3.6\%.$$

Problem 2: Solution: 38.4%.

There are a total $(10-2) \times (10-2) \times (5-2) = 192$ 1 by 1 cubes with no chocolate on them. There are total $10 \times 10 \times 5 = 500$ one by one cubes. Therefore, $\frac{192}{500} = 38.4$ percent of the cubes have no chocolate on them.

Problem 3: Solution: 125.

If all the sides are painted, the number of cubes without any paint will be $(n-2)^3$, which is a cubic number. Since 45 is not a cubic number, we need to find the biggest cubic number that is smaller than 45, which is 27.

So we have $(n-2)^3 = 27$ and $n = 5$.

The total number of unit cubes is then $n^3 = 5^3 = 125$.

Problem 4: Solution: 1/6.

The total number of cubes is 24, which will be the denominator of our fraction. The numerator will be the number of cubes with 0 face painted and the number of cubes with 1 face painted.

From the formulas in the table, we have

$(2-2)(3-2)(4-2) = 0$ cubes with 0 faces painted, and

$2(m-2)(n-2) + 2(m-2)(r-2) + 2(n-2)(r-2) = 2(2-2)(3-2) + 2(2-2)(4-2) + 2(4-2)(3-2) = 4$.

The probability that a randomly selected unit cube will have fewer than two painted faces

is $\frac{4}{24} = \frac{1}{6}$.

Example 1: (1999 Mathcounts Chapter) In the prime factorization of 40!, how many times does the factor 5 occur?

Solution: 9.

Method 1:
First we know 40! means factorial, which means $40 \times 39 \times 38 \times \ldots \times 1$. Since every 5th number has a factor of 5, we start with $40 \div 5 = 8$. There are 8 numbers that have a factor of 5. However, if a number has a factor of 25, it has 2 factors of 5. Every 5th factor of 5 would then also be a factor of 25, so we can divide 8 by 5 to get 1.6. So there is 1 additional factor of 5. There are $8 + 1 = 9$ factors of 5 in 40!. Therefore it ends in 9 zeros.

Method 2:
$$\left\lfloor \frac{40}{5^1} \right\rfloor + \left\lfloor \frac{40}{5^2} \right\rfloor = 8 + \lfloor 1.6 \rfloor = 8 + 1 = 9 .$$

THEOREM:

(1). Theorem: In the prime factorization of $n!$, the number of times the factor m occur is $N = \left\lfloor \dfrac{n}{m^1} \right\rfloor + \left\lfloor \dfrac{n}{m^2} \right\rfloor + \left\lfloor \dfrac{n}{m^3} \right\rfloor + \left\lfloor \dfrac{n}{m^4} \right\rfloor + \ldots$

(2). To find how many zeros $n!$ end is the same as to find N, the number of times the factor 5 occurs in the prime factorization of $n!$.

$\lfloor x \rfloor$ is called the floor function. Whenever we see this notation, we take the greatest integer value not greater than x. For examples: $\lfloor 3.14 \rfloor = 3$, $\lfloor 4.5 \rfloor = 4$.

Example 2: (2002 Mathcounts National Target) In how many zeros does the decimal representation of the number 2002! end?

Solution: 499.

Since in order to end in zero, a number must be divisible by $10 = 5 \times 2$, each zero is the result of the number having a factor of both 5 and 2. Since every other number is even there are plenty of 2's as factors, so we need to see how many factors of 5 there are.

We use the above formula below to find the number of zeros 2002! ends in:

$$N = [\frac{2002}{5}] + [\frac{2002}{5^2}] + [\frac{2002}{5^3}] + [\frac{2002}{5^4}] = 400 + 80 + 16 + 3 = 499.$$

2002! ends in 499 zeros.

Example 3: (2002 NC Math Contest) If one-hundred factorial (100!) base 10 is converted to base 6, how many zeroes will be at the end of the base 6 numeral?

Solution: 48.

Method 1:

In base ten a zero will occur every time there are factors of 5 and 2. Two zeros would result when factors of 25 and 4 are present. Three zeroes would result when 125 and 8 are present, etc. Likewise, in base six, there will be a zero for each 3×2, two zeroes for $3^2 \times 2^2$, etc. In 100 there are: 33 factors of 3, 3 factors of 27, 11 factors of 9, and 1 factor of 81. Total 48 zeros.

Method 2:

$$\left\lfloor \frac{100}{3} \right\rfloor + \left\lfloor \frac{100}{3^2} \right\rfloor + \left\lfloor \frac{100}{3^3} \right\rfloor + \left\lfloor \frac{100}{3^4} \right\rfloor = 33 + 11 + 3 + 1 = 48.$$

Example 4: (1995 National Sprint) How many zeros appear at the end of the whole-number representation of $\frac{20!}{10^4}$?

Solution: 0.

There are n zeros at the end of 20! and $n = \left\lfloor \frac{20}{5} \right\rfloor = 4$. There are 4 zeros for 10^4. The desired solution is then $4 - 4 = 0$.

PROBLEMS:

Problem 1: (1992 National Sprint) In how many zeros does 50! end when expressed in standard base ten notation?

Problem 2: Find how many zeros does 238! end in?

Problem 3: (1970 AMC). The number 10! (10 is written in base 10), when written in the base 12 system, ends with exactly k zeros. The value of k is
(A). 1   (B) 2   (C) 3   (D) 4   (E) 5.

Problem 4: (1992 National Target) In how many zeros does the following end when expressed in standard base ten notation: $\dfrac{50!}{19!\cdot 31!}$?

SOLUTIONS:

Problem 1: Solution:

To find the number of zeros 50! ends in: $\left\lfloor \dfrac{50}{5} \right\rfloor + \left\lfloor \dfrac{50}{5^2} \right\rfloor = 10 + 2 = 12$.

Problem 2: Solution:

Each product of 5×2 will generate a zero. There are more factors of 2 than that of 5. So we just need to look at the number of 5 in the expansion of 238!.

$$\left\lfloor \frac{238}{5} \right\rfloor + \left\lfloor \frac{238}{5^2} \right\rfloor + \left\lfloor \frac{238}{5^3} \right\rfloor = 47 + 9 + 1 = 57$$

Therefore it ends in 57 zeros.

Problem 3: Solution: 4.

Method 1:

In base 10, $10! = 1 \times 2 \times 3 \times 4 \times 5 \times 6 \times 7 \times 8 \times 9 \times 10 = 2^8 \times 3^4 \times 5^2 \times 7 = 12^4 \times 5^2 \times 7$.

and $5^2 \times 7 = 175 = 1 \times 12^2 + 2 \times 12 + 7$.

Thus $(5^2 \times 7 \times 14^4)_{10} = (127 \times 10^4)_{12} = 1{,}270{,}000_{12}$

This number ends with exactly 4 zeros.

Method 2:

Since $12 = 3 \times 4$. Each product of 3×4 will generate a zero in base 12 system. There are more factor of 4 than the factor of 3. We just look at the number of factor of 3.

The number of tailing zeros is $\left\lfloor \dfrac{10}{3} \right\rfloor + \left\lfloor \dfrac{10}{3^2} \right\rfloor = 3 + 1 = 4$.

Problem 4: (1992 National Target)

Solution:

There are $\left\lfloor \dfrac{50}{5} \right\rfloor + \left\lfloor \dfrac{50}{5^2} \right\rfloor = 10 + 2 = 12$ zeros in 50! and $\left\lfloor \dfrac{19}{5} \right\rfloor = 3$ zeros in 19!

There are $\left\lfloor \dfrac{31}{5} \right\rfloor + \left\lfloor \dfrac{31}{5^2} \right\rfloor = 6 + 1 = 7$ zeros in 31!

The solution is 2 (zeros): $\dfrac{10^{12}}{10^3 \times 10^7} = 10^2$.

Example 1: (Mathcounts Handbook) Express 42_{five} as a base ten numeral.

Solution: 22.

$4 \times 5^1 + 2 \times 5^0 = 22$.

Any positive integer N can be expressed as the polynomial of p:

$$N = a_n p^n + a_{n-1} p^{n-1} + \ldots + a_0 p^0$$

where a_n, $a_{n-1}, \ldots,$ and a_0 can be any one of 0, 1, 2, 3,..., $(p-1)$, n is a nonnegative integer and p represents the base.

Expansion method to convert a number from another base form to base 10.

Convert xyz in base b to base 10.

$$xyx_b = xb^2 + yb^1 + zb^0$$

Example 2: (Mathcounts Handbook) Express the base ten numeral 26 as a base three numeral.

Solution: 222.

$10_{10} = (3 + 3 + 3 + 1)_{10} = (10 + 10 + 10 + 1)_3 + 1_3 = (101)_3$.
$3_{10} = 10_3$.
$26_{10} = 10_{10} + 10_{10} + 3_{10} + 3_{10} = 101_3 + 101_3 + 10_3 + 10_3 = = 222_3$.

Example 3: Express 32_{seven} in base eight.

Solution: 27_{eight}.

(1) Convert this number from base b to base 10: $32_7 = 3 \times 7^1 + 2 \times 7^0 = 23_{10}$

(2) Next, convert the base 10 number to base 8: $23_{10} = 8 + 8 + 7 = 10_8 + 10_8 + 7 = 27_8$.

Combined method to convert a number from base b to base c

(1) Convert this number from base b to base 10
(2) Next, convert the base 10 number to base c.

Example 4: The following multiplication problem is correctly done if the numbers are in base b. $15 \times 15 = 321$. What is b?

Solution: 6.

The given equation can be written in base b as:
$(1 \times b + 5) \times (1 \times b + 5) = 3 \times b^2 + 2b + 1 \Rightarrow b^2 - 4b - 12 = 0 \Rightarrow (b-6)(b+4) = 0$.
Solving we get $b = 6$ and $b = -4$ (ignored).

Example 5: Our number system is base 10, perhaps because we have ten fingers. In another world, the inhabitants have a different number of fingers (y) and they use a base y number system. Here are two examples of problems in this other would: $4 \times 6 = 30$, and $4 \times 7 = 34$. What is the value of $4 \times 5 \times 7$ expressed in the number system of this other would?

Solution: 214.

From $4 \times 6 = 30$, we get $4 \times 6 = 3 \times b \Rightarrow b = 8$.
$(4 \times 5 \times 7)_{10} = 140_{10} = [(8+2)(8+6)]_{10} = [(10+2)(10+6)]_8 = [12 \times 16]_8 = 214_8$.

Example 6: The three-digit base-six number, nmn_6, is equal to the product of 23_4 and 34_5. What digit is represented by n?

Solution: 5.

$n \times 6^2 + m \times 6^1 + n = (2 \times 4^1 + 3)(3 \times 5^1 + 4) \Rightarrow 37n + 6m = 209$.
Solving we get $n = 5$.

PROBLEMS

Problem 1: Express 35_{seven} as a base ten numeral. (Mathcounts Competitions).

Problem 2: Express 125_{ten} as a base eight number.

Problem 3: Convert 1342_{five} to base three.

Problem 4: 792_b is divisible by 297_b. What is the value of base b?

Problem 5: Find the sum of the values of A and B which make the following statement true: $23B1_{four} = 2AB_{nine}$.

Problem 6: (Mathcounts Competitions) For what positive integral base b does $21_b \times 54_b = 1354_b$?

Problem 7: For what value(s) of t will the five-digit number $\underline{23t42}_6$ be divisible by 5?

SOLUTION

Problem 1: Solution: 26.

$3 \times 7^1 + 5 \times 7^0 = 26$.

Problem 2: Solution: 175_8.

$125_{10} = (15 \times 8 + 5)_{10} = [(8 + 7) \times 8 + 5)]_{10} = [(10 + 7) \times 10 + 5)]_8$
$= [(17) \times 10 + 5)]_8 = 175_8$.

Problem 3: Solution: 2220_3.

We first convert this number to base 10 and then convert the base 10 to base 5:

$1342_{\text{five}} = 1 \times 5^3 + 3 \times 5^2 + 4 \times 5^1 + 2 \times 5^0 = 222_{10}$.

Next, we convert 222 from base 10 to base 3:

$222_{10} = 6 \times (6 \times 6 + 1)_{10} = [20 \times (20 \times 20 + 1)]_3 = [20 \times (110 + 1)]_3$
$= [2200 + 20]_3 = 2220_3$.

Problem 4: Solution: 19.

The number contains a digit 9, so the base is at least 10. In such a base, the following is true:

$2 \times 297 < 792 < 4 \times 297$.

So $792_b = 3 \times 297_b$.

$7b^2 + 9b + 2 = 3(2b^2 + 9b + 7) \qquad \Rightarrow \qquad b^2 - 18b - 19 = 0 \qquad \Rightarrow \qquad b = 19$.

Problem 5: Solution: 3.

$2 \times 4^3 + 3 \times 4^2 + 4B + 1 = 2 \times 9^2 + 9A + B$
$177 + 4B = 162 + 9A + B \qquad \Rightarrow \qquad 3A = 5 + B$
$B = 1$ and $A = 2$
$A + B = 3$.

Problem 6: Solution: 8.

$(2b + 1)(5b + 4) = b^3 + 3b^2 + 5b + 4 \qquad \Rightarrow \qquad b^3 - 7b^2 - 8b = 0 \Rightarrow b(b^2 - 7b - 8) = 0$

We know that b $\neq$ 0 so we have $(b^2 - 7b - 8) = 0$ $\Rightarrow$ $(b-8)(b+1) = 0$.
$b = 8$, $b = -1$ (ignored).

Problem 7: Solution: 4.
We first convert the given number to base 10:
$$\overline{23t42}\,_6 = 2 \times 6^4 + 3 \times 6^3 + t \times 6^2 + 4 \times 6^1 + 2 \times 6^0$$

If the number is divisible by 5, we have:
$$2 \times 6^4 + 3 \times 6^3 + t \times 6^2 + 4 \times 6^1 + 2 \times 6^0$$
$2 \times 1^4 + 3 \times 1^3 + t \times 1^2 + 4 \times 1^1 + 2 = t + 1$ divisible by 5. So $t = 4$.

Example 1: (1996 Mathcounts Handbook) Find positive integers x and y, how many ordered pairs (x, y) satisfy $xy + x - y = 53$?

Solution: 5.

$xy + x - y = (x-1)(y+1) + 1 = 53$ $\Rightarrow$ $(x-1)(y+1) = 52 = 1 \times 52 = 4 \times 13 = 2 \times 26$.

So we have:

Case I: $(x-1) = 1$ and $(y+1) = 52$ $\Rightarrow$ (2, 51).

Case II: $(x-1) = 4$ and $(y+1) = 13$ $\Rightarrow$ (5, 12).

Case III: $(x-1) = 13$ and $(y+1) = 4$ $\Rightarrow$ (14, 3).

Case IV: $(x-1) = 2$ and $(y+1) = 26$ $\Rightarrow$ (3, 25).

Case V: $(x-1) = 26$ and $(y+1) = 2$ $\Rightarrow$ (27, 1).

Note: $(x-1) = 52$ and $(y+1) = 1$ do not yield positive integer solutions.

$$ab + a + b + 1 = (a+1)(b+1)$$
$$ab - a + b - 1 = (a+1)(b-1)$$
$$ab + a - b - 1 = (a-1)(b+1)$$
$$ab - a - b + 1 = (a-1)(b-1)$$

$$abc + ab + bc + ac + a + b + c + 1 = (a+1)(b+1)(c+1)$$
$$abc + ab - bc + ac + a - b - c - 1 = (a-1)(b+1)(c+1)$$
$$abc + ab - bc - ac - a - b + c + 1 = (a-1)(b-1)(c+1)$$
$$abc - ab - bc - ac + a + b + c - 1 = (a-1)(b-1)(c-1)$$

Example 2: (Mathcounts) How many pairs (a, b), where a and b are positive integers and $a > b$, satisfy the equation $\dfrac{1}{a} + \dfrac{1}{b} = \dfrac{1}{8}$?

Solution: 3 pairs.

$8b + 8a = ab \quad \Rightarrow \quad (a-8)(b-8) = 64 = 1 \times 64 = 2 \times 32 = 4 \times 16 = 8 \times 8$.

So we have:

Case I: $a - 8 = 1$ and $b - 8 = 64$ $\Rightarrow$ (9, 72).

Case II: $a - 8 = 2$ and $b - 8 = 32$ $\Rightarrow$ (10, 40).

Case III: $a - 8 = 4$ and $b - 8 = 16$ $\Rightarrow$ (12, 24).

Case IV: $a - 8 = 8$ and $b - 8 = 8$ $\Rightarrow$ (16, 16) ignored since $a = b$.

Example 3: (1995 Mathcounts State Competition) Find the sum of the x-coordinates of all possible integral solutions to $\dfrac{1}{x} + \dfrac{1}{y} = \dfrac{1}{7}$.

Solution: 78.

The equation can be re-written as $xy - 7x - 7y = 0$ or $(x-7)(y-7) = 49$.

$$\begin{cases} (x-7) = 1, & -1, & 7, & -7, & 49, & -49 \\ (y-7) = 49, & -49, & 7, & -7, & 1, & -1 \end{cases}$$

We have the solutions $\begin{cases} x = 8, & 6, & 14, & 0, & 56, & -42 \\ y = 56, & 42, & 14, & 0, & 81, & 6 \end{cases}$

The sum of the x-coordinates of all positive integral solutions is $8 + 14 + 56 = 78$.

Example 4: (1994 Mathcounts National Sprint) Given the equation $\dfrac{1}{m} + \dfrac{1}{n} = \dfrac{2}{15}$, where m and n are positive integers, find the value of $m + n$ such that $m > n$ and m is not a multiple of n.

Solution: 32.

We re-write the equation as $2mn = 15m + 15n$ $\Rightarrow$ $4mn = 30m + 30n$ $\Rightarrow$

$(2m - 15)(2n - 15) = 225 = 225 \times 1 = 75 \times 3 = 45 \times 5 = 25 \times 9 = 15 \times 15$.

So we have:

Case I: $2m - 15 = 225$ and $2n - 15 = 1$ $\Rightarrow$ (120, 8).

Case II: $2m - 15 = 75$ and $2n - 15 = 3$ $\Rightarrow$ (45, 9).

Case III: $2m - 15 = 45$ and $2n - 15 = 5$ $\Rightarrow$ (30, 15).

Case IV: $2m-15=25$ and $2n-15=9$ $\Rightarrow$ (20, 12).
Case IV: $2m-15=15$ and $2n-15=15$ $\Rightarrow$ (15, 15).
The only case where m is not a multiple of n is case IV. So $m + n = 20 + 12 = 32$.

Example 5: Find n, the number of all nonnegative integer solutions to the equation $xyz + xy + xz + yz + x + y + z = 213$.

Solution: 9.

The given equation can be written as $(x+1)(y+1)(z+1) = 214$.
$214 = 1 \times 1 \times 214 = 1 \times 2 \times 107$.

Without loss of generality, let $x \geq y \geq z$

$$\begin{cases} x+1=214 \\ y+1=1 \\ z+1=1 \end{cases} \Rightarrow \quad x=213, \quad y=0, \quad z=0$$

$$\begin{cases} x+1=102 \\ y+1=2 \\ z+1=1 \end{cases} \Rightarrow \quad x=101, \quad y=1, \quad z=0$$

Based on the property of symmetry, we have all the solutions of (x, y, z):
(213, 0, 0), (0, 213, 0), (0, 0, 213);
(101, 1, 0), (101, 0, 1), (1, 101, 0), (1, 0, 101), (0, 101, 1), (0, 1, 101).

There are a total of 9.

PROBLEMS

Problem 1: (Mathcounts Handbook) How many ordered pairs of positive integers (x, y) satisfy $x + y + xy = 63$?

Problem 2: (1999 Mathcounts National Team Round) Given positive integers x and y such that $x \neq y$ and $\dfrac{1}{x} + \dfrac{1}{y} = \dfrac{1}{12}$, what is the smallest possible value for $x + y$?

Problem 3: (AMC) How many ordered pairs (m, n) of positive integers are solutions to $\dfrac{4}{m} + \dfrac{2}{n} = 1$?

Problem 4: What is the product of positive integers a and b such that $a > b$ and $\dfrac{1}{a} + \dfrac{1}{b} + \dfrac{1}{ab} = 1$?

Problem 5: Factor: $1 + a + b + c + ab + bc + ac + abc$.

Problem 6: a, b, and c are positive integers, find $(a+1)(b+1)(c+1)$ if $ab + a + b = bc + b + c = ac + a + c = 3$.

SOLUTIONS

Problem 1: Solution: 3 pairs.

$xy + x + y = (x+1)(y+1) - 1 = 63 \quad \Rightarrow$

$\quad\quad (x+1)(y+1) = 64 = 1 \times 64 = 2 \times 32 = 4 \times 16 = 8 \times 8$.

So we have:

Case I: $(x+1) = 1$ and $(y+1) = 64 \quad\quad \Rightarrow \quad\quad$ (0, 63) ignored.

Case II: $(x+1) = 2$ and $(y+1) = 32 \quad\quad \Rightarrow \quad\quad$ (1, 31).

Case III: $(x+1) = 4$ and $(y+1) = 16 \quad\quad \Rightarrow \quad\quad$ (3, 15).

Case IV: $(x+1) = 8$ and $(y+1) = 8 \quad\quad \Rightarrow \quad\quad$ (7, 7).

Problem 2: Solution: 49.

The given equation can be written as: $12y + 12x = xy$, or

$xy - 12x - 12x = 0 \quad \Rightarrow \quad (x-12)(y-12) = 144$

We know that the smallest value for $x + y$ can be obtained when x and y are as close as possible. Since $x \neq y$, we are not able to have $(x-12)(y-12) = 12 \times 12$ but

$(x-12)(y-12) = 9 \times 16$.

Let $y - 12 = 9$ (or 16), then $y = 21$ and $x = 28$. Therefore $28 + 21 = 49$ is the desired solution.

Problem 3: Solution: 4.

Since m and n must both be positive, it follows that $n > 2$ and $m > 4$.

$\dfrac{4}{m} + \dfrac{2}{n} = 1$ can be written as: $(m-4)(n-2) = 8$.

We only need to find all the ways of writing 8 as a product of positive integers.

The 4 ways are (1, 8), (2, 4), (4, 2), and (8, 1) corresponding to 4 solutions, $(m, n) = $ (5,10), (6,6), (8, 4), and (12, 3).

Problem 4: Solution: 6.

The given equation can be written as $b + a + 1 = ab$ or

$ab - a - b = 1 \quad\quad \Rightarrow \quad\quad (a-1)(b-1) = 2$.

We have $(a-1) = 2$ and $(b-1) = 1$.

So $a = 3$ and $b\ a = 2$. The product is 6.

Problem 5: Solution:

$1 + a + b + c + ab + bc + ac + abc = (1+c) + b(1+c) + (a + ab + ac + abc)$

$= (1+c) + b(1+c) + a(1+b+c+bc) = (1+b)(1+c) + a(1+b)(1+c)$

$= (1+a)(1+b)(1+c)$.

Problem 6: Solution: 8.

$ab + a + b = 3$	$\Rightarrow$	$(a+1)(b+1) = 4$	(1)
$bc + b + c = 3$	$\Rightarrow$	$(b+1)(c+1) = 4$	(2)
$ac + a + c = 3$	$\Rightarrow$	$(c+1)(a+1) = 4$	(3)

$(1) \times (2) \times (3)$: $[(a+1)(b+1)(c+1)]^2 = 64$.

Since a, b, and c are positive integers, $(a+1)(b+1)(c+1) = 8$.

Example 1: (2009 Mathcounts State Sprint/2010 Mathcounts Handbook) If $1 \le a \le 10$ and $1 \le b \le 36$, for how many ordered pairs of integers (a, b) is $\sqrt{a + \sqrt{b}}$ an integer?

Solution:

Since $\sqrt{a + \sqrt{b}}$ is an integer, we let $\sqrt{a + \sqrt{b}} = n$.

Squaring both sides: $a + \sqrt{b} = n^2$.

Since $\sqrt{a + \sqrt{b}}$ is an integer, $\sqrt{b}$ must be an integer and b is a square number.

The possible values of b are 1, 4, 9, 16, 25, and 36.

The possible values of $\sqrt{b}$ are 1, 2, 3, 4, 5, and 6.

So we see that

$a + 1 = n^2$ and a can be 3 and 8.

$a + 2 = n^2$ and a can be 2 and 7.

$a + 3 = n^2$ and a can be 1 and 6.

$a + 4 = n^2$ and a can be 5 only.

$a + 5 = n^2$ and a can be 4 only.

$a + 6 = n^2$ and a can be 3 and 10.

We get 10 ordered pairs.

Example 2: (2006 National) The number $\sqrt{17 + 12\sqrt{2}}$ is an example of a number expressed in "embedded radical form" because of the $\sqrt{2}$ under the radical. What is the equivalent value of this number expressed in simplest radical form $a + b\sqrt{c}$ where a and b are integers and c is a positive integer containing no perfect square factors greater than 1?

Solution:

Method 1

$$\sqrt{17 + 12\sqrt{2}} = \sqrt{3^2 + 2 \times 3 \times \sqrt{8} + (\sqrt{8})^2} = \sqrt{(3 + \sqrt{8})^2} = 3 + \sqrt{8} = 3 + 2\sqrt{2}.$$

Method 2

Let $\sqrt{17 + 12\sqrt{2}} = \sqrt{a} + \sqrt{b}$.

Square both sides: $17 + 12\sqrt{2} = a + 2\sqrt{ab} + b \Rightarrow a + b = 17$ and $ab = 72$.
$a = 9$ and $b = 8$.
$$\sqrt{17 + 12\sqrt{2}} = \sqrt{9} + \sqrt{8} = 3 + 2\sqrt{2}.$$

Method 3:

We write $\sqrt{17 + 12\sqrt{2}}$ as $\sqrt{17 + \sqrt{288}}$. We then use the following formula:

$$\sqrt{a + \sqrt{b}} = \sqrt{\frac{17 + \sqrt{17^2 - 288}}{2}} + \sqrt{\frac{17 - \sqrt{17^2 - 288}}{2}} = \sqrt{\frac{17 + 1}{2}} + \sqrt{\frac{17 - 1}{2}} = 3 + 2\sqrt{2}.$$

A nested radical is a radical expression that contains another radical expression.

Some nested radicals can be rewritten in a form that is not nested. Rewriting a nested radical in this way is called **denesting**.

Radical Theorem: $\sqrt{a + \sqrt{b}}$ can be denested if and only if

$a > 0, b > 0$ (1)

and $a^2 - b = k^2$ $(k > 0)$ (2)

Denesting formulas:

$$\sqrt{a \pm \sqrt{b}} = \sqrt{\frac{a + \sqrt{a^2 - b}}{2}} \pm \sqrt{\frac{a - \sqrt{a^2 - b}}{2}}.$$

$$\sqrt{a \pm \sqrt{b}} = \frac{\sqrt{2}}{2}\left(\sqrt{a + \sqrt{a^2 - b}} \pm \sqrt{a - \sqrt{a^2 - b}}\right).$$

$$\sqrt{a \pm \sqrt{b}} = \sqrt{\frac{4a \pm 4\sqrt{b}}{4}} = \frac{1}{2}\sqrt{4a \pm 2\sqrt{4b}}.$$

Example 3: Simplify $\sqrt{3+2\sqrt{2}}$

Solution:

Method 1: $\sqrt{3+2\sqrt{2}} = \sqrt{2+2\sqrt{2}+1} = \sqrt{(\sqrt{2})^2 + 2\sqrt{2}\times 1 + 1^2} = \sqrt{(\sqrt{2}+1)^2} = \sqrt{2}+1$

Method 2: $\sqrt{3+2\sqrt{2}} = \sqrt{3+\sqrt{8}} = \sqrt{\dfrac{3+\sqrt{3^2-8}}{2}} + \sqrt{\dfrac{3-\sqrt{3^2-8}}{2}} = \sqrt{\dfrac{4}{2}} + \sqrt{\dfrac{2}{2}} = \sqrt{2}+1$

Example 4: Simplify $\sqrt{7-\sqrt{24}}$

Solution:

$\sqrt{7-\sqrt{24}} = \sqrt{7-2\sqrt{6}} = \sqrt{6-2\sqrt{6}+1} = \sqrt{(\sqrt{6})^2 - 2\sqrt{6}\times 1 + 1^2} = \sqrt{(\sqrt{6}-1)^2} = \sqrt{6}-1$

Case I: If $\sqrt{a\pm 2\sqrt{b}} = \sqrt{x} \pm \sqrt{y}$, $(x > 0, y > 0, x > y)$, then $a \pm 2\sqrt{b} = x + y \pm 2\sqrt{xy}$.

Case II: If we can find x, y $(x > y)$, such that $x + y = a$, $xy = b$, then $\sqrt{a\pm 2\sqrt{b}} = \sqrt{x} \pm \sqrt{y}$.

Example 5: Simplify $\sqrt{11+2\sqrt{18}}$.

Solution:

We can rewrite the given radical as $\sqrt{11+2\sqrt{18}} = \sqrt{11+\sqrt{72}}$.

We see that $a = 11$, $b = 72$, and $a^2 - b = 11^2 - 72 = 49 = 7^2$. (5.1) and (5.2) are both satisfied. Therefore the given nested radical can be denested.

Let $\sqrt{11+2\sqrt{18}} = \sqrt{x} + \sqrt{y}$.

Squaring both sides: $11 + 2\sqrt{18} = x + y + 2\sqrt{xy}$.

Solving we get $\begin{cases} x+y=11 \\ xy=18. \end{cases}$ $\Rightarrow$ $\begin{cases} x=2 \\ y=9 \end{cases}$ or $\begin{cases} x=9 \\ y=2 \end{cases}$.

$$\sqrt{11+2\sqrt{18}} = \sqrt{9} + \sqrt{2} = 3 + \sqrt{2}$$

Example 6: (2011 AMC 10A) Which of the following is equal to $\sqrt{9-6\sqrt{2}}$ + $\sqrt{9+6\sqrt{2}}$?

(A) $3\sqrt{2}$ (B) $2\sqrt{6}$ (C) $\dfrac{7\sqrt{2}}{2}$ (D) $3\sqrt{3}$ 3 (E) 6.

Solution: (B).

We can rewrite the given radical as $\sqrt{9+6\sqrt{2}} = \sqrt{9+\sqrt{72}}$.

We see that $a = 9$, $b = 72$, and $a^2 - b = 9^2 - 72 = 9 = 3^2$. Therefore the given nested radical can be denested.

Method 1: By the formula, we have

$$\sqrt{9+\sqrt{72}} = \sqrt{\frac{9+\sqrt{9^2-72}}{2}} + \sqrt{\frac{9-\sqrt{9^2-72}}{2}} = \sqrt{6}+\sqrt{3}.$$

Similarly, $\sqrt{9-6\sqrt{2}} = \sqrt{9-\sqrt{72}} = \sqrt{\frac{9+\sqrt{9^2-72}}{2}} - \sqrt{\frac{9-\sqrt{9^2-72}}{2}} = \sqrt{6}-\sqrt{3}$.

Thus $\sqrt{9-6\sqrt{2}} + \sqrt{9+6\sqrt{2}} = \sqrt{6}+\sqrt{3}+\sqrt{6}-\sqrt{3} = 2\sqrt{6}$.

Method 2:

$$\sqrt{9-6\sqrt{2}} = \sqrt{9-2\sqrt{18}} = \sqrt{6-2\sqrt{18}+3} = \sqrt{(\sqrt{6})^2 - 2\sqrt{6}\times\sqrt{3} + (\sqrt{3})^2} = \sqrt{6}-\sqrt{3}$$

Similarly, $\sqrt{9+6\sqrt{2}} = \sqrt{6}+\sqrt{3}$.

Thus $\sqrt{9-6\sqrt{2}} + \sqrt{9+6\sqrt{2}} = \sqrt{6}+\sqrt{3}+\sqrt{6}-\sqrt{3} = 2\sqrt{6}$.

PROBLEMS

Problem 1: Simplify $\sqrt{3 - 2\sqrt{2}}$

Problem 2: Simplify $\sqrt{7 + \sqrt{24}}$

Problem 3: Simplify $\sqrt{4 + 2\sqrt{3}}$.

Problem 4: Simplify $\sqrt{2 - \sqrt{3}}$.

Problem 5: Simplify $\sqrt{6 - \sqrt{11}} + \sqrt{6 + \sqrt{11}}$.

Problem 6: Simplify $\sqrt{4 + \sqrt{7}} - \sqrt{4 - \sqrt{7}}$.

Problem 7: If $1 \le a \le 10$ and $1 \le b \le 100$, for how many ordered pairs of integers (a, b) can $\sqrt{a + \sqrt{b}}$ be expressed as the form of $x + \sqrt{y}$, where both x and y are positive integers?

SOLUTIONS

Problem 1: Solution:

$$\sqrt{3-2\sqrt{2}} = \sqrt{2-2\sqrt{2}+1} = \sqrt{(\sqrt{2})^2 - 2\sqrt{2}\times 1 + 1^2} = \sqrt{(\sqrt{2}-1)^2} = \sqrt{2}-1$$

Problem 2: Solution:

$$\sqrt{7+\sqrt{24}} = \sqrt{7+2\sqrt{6}} = \sqrt{6+2\sqrt{6}+1} = \sqrt{(\sqrt{6})^2 + 2\sqrt{6}\times 1 + 1^2} = \sqrt{(\sqrt{6}+1)^2} = \sqrt{6}+1$$

Problem 3: Solution:

We rewrite the given radical as $\sqrt{4+2\sqrt{3}} = \sqrt{4+\sqrt{12}}$.

Let $a = 4$, $b = 12$.
$a^2 - b = 4^2 - 12 = 4 = 2^2$.

The given nested radical can be denested:

$$\sqrt{4\pm 2\sqrt{3}} = \sqrt{(3+1)+2\sqrt{3\times 1}} = \sqrt{(\sqrt{3}+1)^2} = \sqrt{3}+1.$$

Problem 4: Solution:
Method 1:

$$\sqrt{2-\sqrt{3}} = \sqrt{\frac{8-2\sqrt{12}}{4}} = \frac{1}{2}\sqrt{8-2\sqrt{12}} = \frac{\sqrt{6}-\sqrt{2}}{2}.$$

Method 2:

$$\sqrt{2-\sqrt{3}} = \sqrt{\frac{2+\sqrt{2^2-3}}{2}} - \sqrt{\frac{2-\sqrt{2^2-3}}{2}} = \sqrt{\frac{3}{2}} - \sqrt{\frac{1}{2}} = \frac{\sqrt{6}-\sqrt{2}}{2}.$$

Problem 5: Solution: $\sqrt{22}$.
We see that $a = 6$, $b = 11$, and $a^2 - b = 6^2 - 11 = 25 = 5^2$. Therefore the given nested radical can be denested.
By the formula, we have

$$\sqrt{6+\sqrt{11}} = \sqrt{\frac{6+\sqrt{6^2-11}}{2}} + \sqrt{\frac{6-\sqrt{6^2-11}}{2}} = \sqrt{\frac{11}{2}} + \sqrt{\frac{1}{2}}.$$

Similarly, $\sqrt{6-\sqrt{11}} = \sqrt{\dfrac{6+\sqrt{6^2-11}}{2}} - \sqrt{\dfrac{6-\sqrt{6^2-11}}{2}} = \sqrt{\dfrac{11}{2}} - \sqrt{\dfrac{1}{2}}$.

Thus $\sqrt{6-\sqrt{11}} + \sqrt{6+\sqrt{11}} = \sqrt{\dfrac{11}{2}} + \sqrt{\dfrac{1}{2}} + \sqrt{\dfrac{11}{2}} - \sqrt{\dfrac{1}{2}} = 2\sqrt{\dfrac{11}{2}} = 2\sqrt{\dfrac{2\times11}{2\times2}} = \sqrt{22}$.

Problem 6: Solution: $\sqrt{2}$.

We see that $a = 4$, $b = 7$, and $a^2 - b = 4^2 - 7 = 9 = 3^2$. Therefore the given nested radical can be denested.

By the formula, we have

$\sqrt{4+\sqrt{7}} = \sqrt{\dfrac{4+\sqrt{4^2-7}}{2}} + \sqrt{\dfrac{4-\sqrt{4^2-7}}{2}} = \sqrt{\dfrac{7}{2}} + \sqrt{\dfrac{1}{2}}$.

Similarly, $\sqrt{4-\sqrt{7}} = \sqrt{\dfrac{4+\sqrt{4^2-7}}{2}} - \sqrt{\dfrac{4-\sqrt{4^2-7}}{2}} = \sqrt{\dfrac{7}{2}} - \sqrt{\dfrac{1}{2}}$.

Thus $\sqrt{4+\sqrt{7}} - \sqrt{4-\sqrt{7}} = \sqrt{\dfrac{7}{2}} + \sqrt{\dfrac{1}{2}} - (\sqrt{\dfrac{7}{2}} - \sqrt{\dfrac{1}{2}}) = 2\dfrac{1}{\sqrt{2}} = \sqrt{2}$.

Problem 7: Solution: 45.

Since $\sqrt{a+\sqrt{b}}$ can be expressed as $x + \sqrt{y}$ if and only if $a^2 - b = k^2$, $(k > 0)$.

When $a = 10$, we have $100 - b = k^2$. k can be 1, 2, 3.., 9.

When $a = 9$, we have $81 - b = k^2$. k can be 1, 2, 3.., 8.

……

When $a = 2$, we have $4 - b = k^2$. k can be 1 only.

There are $9 + 8 + … + 1 = 45$ values for k. Thus there are 45 pairs of (a, b).

Example 1: We have a two-pan balance scale comes with two weights: 1 gram and 2 grams. (a) If these weights can only be put in one pan during a weighing, how many different weighable values are there? (b) If these weights can be put in in either or both pans during a weighing, how many different weighable values are there?

Solution:

(a) If we only use one weight during each measurement, we are able to measure things weighing 1 gram or 2 grams. If we put both 1 gram and 2 grams weights together in one pan, we can measure things with $1 + 2 = 3$ grams. So we get 3 weighable values: 1, 2, and 3.

(b) We know from (a) that we can get 3 weighable values: 1, 2, and 3. If we put 1 gram weight in one pan and 2 grams weight in another pan, we can measure things weighting $2 - 1 = 1$ gram which we already have. So we still have 3 weighable values: 1, 2, and 3.

Example 2: We have a two-pan balance scale comes with two weights: 1 gram and 3 grams. (a) If these weights can only be put in one pan during a weighing, how many different weighable values are there? (b) If these weights can be put in either or both pans during a weighing, how many different weighable values are there?

Solution:

(a) If we only use one weight during each measurement, we are able to measure things weighing 1 gram or 3 grams. If we put both 1 gram and 3 grams weights together in one pan, we can measure things with $1 + 3 = 4$ grams. So we get 3 weighable values: 1, 3, and 4.

(b) We know from (a) that we can get 3 weighable values: 1, 3, and 4. If we put 1 gram weight in one pan and 3 grams weight in another pan, we are able to measure things weighting 2 grams. So we have 4 weighable values: 1, 2, 3, and 4.

Example 3: We have a two-pan balance scale comes with two weights: 1 gram and 4 grams. (a) If these weights can only be put in one pan during a weighing, how many different weighable values are there? (b) If these weights can be put in in either or both pans during a weighing, how many different weighable values are there?

Solution:

(a) If we only use one weight during each measurement, we are able to measure things weighing 1 gram or 4 grams. If we put both 1 gram and 4 grams weights together in one pan, we can measure things with $1 + 4 = 5$ grams. So we get 3 weighable values: 1, 4, and 5.

(b) We know from (a) that we can get 3 weighable values: 1, 4, and 5. If we put 1 gram weight in one pan and 4 grams weight in another pan, we are able to measure things weighting 3 gram. So we have 4 weighable values: 1, 3, 4, and 5.

Example 4: We have a two-pan balance scale comes with three weights: 1 gram, 3 grams and 9 grams. (a) If these weights can only be put in one pan during a weighing, how many different weighable values are there? (b) If these weights can be put in in either or both pans during a weighing, how many different weighable values are there?

Solution:

(a) If we only use one weight during each measurement, we are able to measure things weighing 1 gram, 3 grams, or 9 grams. If we use two weights each time, we get 3 weighable values $(1 + 3 = 4, 1 + 9 = 10,$ and $3 + 9 = 12)$. If we use three weights at one time, we get one more weighable value $(1 + 3 + 9 = 13)$. Or in other way:

$$\binom{3}{1} + \binom{3}{2} + \binom{3}{3} = 3 + 3 + 1 = 7.$$

(b) We know from (a) that we can get 7 weighable values: 1, 3, 9, 4, 10, 12, and 13.

If we put 1 gram weight in one pan and 3 grams weight in another pan, we are able to measure things weighting 2 grams.

If we put 1 gram weight in one pan and 9 grams weight in another pan, we are able to measure things weighting 8 grams.

If we put 3 gram weight in one pan and 9 grams weight in another pan, we are able to measure things weighting 6 grams.

If we put 1 gram weight in one pan and 3 and 9 grams weights in another pan, we are able to measure things weighting 11 grams.

If we put 3 grams weight in one pan and 1 and 9 grams weights in another pan, we are able to measure things weighting 7 grams.

If we put 9 grams weight in one pan and 1 and 3 grams weights in another pan, we are able to measure things weighting 5 grams.

So we have $7 + 6 = 13$ weighable values: 1 up to 13.

THEOREM 1: There is n number of different weights.

(a). If the weights can only be put to one side of the scale, the greatest number of weighable values is $2^n - 1$.

n	1	2	3	4	5	6 .... n
greatest number of weighable values:	1	3	7	15	31	63...., $2^n - 1$.

(b). If the weights are $2^0, 2^1, 2^2, 2^3,..., 2^n - 1$, the weighable values are from 1 to $2^n - 1$.

THEOREM 2: There is n number of different weights.

(a). If the weights can be put in both sides of the scale, the greatest number of weighable values is $\dfrac{3^n - 1}{2}$.

n	1	2	3	4	5 .... n
greatest number of weighable values	1	4	13	40	121 ....$\dfrac{3^n - 1}{2}$.

(b). If the weights are $3^0, 3^1, 3^2, 3^3,..., 3^n - 1$, the weighable values are from 1 to $\dfrac{3^n - 1}{2}$.

Problem 1: There are five weighing cubes of 1g, 2g, 4g, 8g, and 16g. How many different values can be weighted if these weights can only be put in one side of the scale during a weighing?

Problem 2: There are five weighing cubes of 1g, 2g, 4g, 8g, and 16g. How many different values can be weighted if these weights can be put in both sides of the scale during a weighing?

Problem 3: (2005 Mathcounts Handbook) A two-pan balance scale comes with a collection of weights. Each weight weighs a whole number of grams. Weights can be put in only one pan during a weighing. To ensure any whole number of grams up to 60 grams can be measured, what is the minimum number of weights needed in the collection?

Problem 4: A two-pan balance scale comes with a collection of weights. Each weight weighs a whole number of grams. Weights can be put in either or both pans during a weighing. To ensure any whole number of grams up to 100 grams can be measured, what is the minimum number of weights needed in the collection?

SOLUTIONS

Problem 1: Solution:
Method 1: By the theorem 1 (a), we know the number of different values is $2^n - 1 = 2^5 - 1 = 31$.

Method 2: Get one, two,… five cubes each time, the resulting sums are different. So know the number of different values is $\binom{5}{1} + \binom{5}{2} + \binom{5}{3} + \binom{5}{4} + \binom{5}{5} = 2^5 - 1 = 31$.

Problem 2: Solution:
By the theorem 1 (a), we know the number of different values is $2^n - 1 = 2^5 - 1 = 31$ if these weights can only be put in side of the scale during a weighing.

We see that the greatest weighable value is $1 + 2 + 4 + 8 + 16 = 31$ and the smallest weighable value is 1. There are 31 whole numbers from 1 to 31. So we still get 31 weighable values even we are allowed to put the weights in both sides of the scale during a weighing.

Problem 3: Solution: 6 weights.
The 6 weights are 1g, 2g, 4g, 8g, 16g, and 32g.

These 6 weights can measure any weight from 1g to up to $2^n - 1 = 2^6 - 1 = 64 - 1 = 63$g.

Problem 4: Solution: 5 weights.
The 5 weights are 1g, 3g, 9g, 27g, and 81g.

These 5 weights can measure any weight from 1g to up to $\dfrac{3^n - 1}{2} = 242/2 = 121$ g.

Example 1: A penny A is rolling around a second penny B without slipping until it returns to its starting point. How many revolutions does *penny A* make?

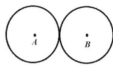

Solution: Two revolutions.

The distance D traveled by the centre of the circle A can be used as a representative distance traveled by the circle A.

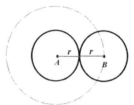

$D = 2\pi(r + r) = 4\pi r.$

The number of revolutions is $\dfrac{4\pi r}{2\pi r} = 2$.

Theorem 1: Circle A is rolling around a second circle B without slipping until it returns to its starting point. The number of revolutions the circle A make is

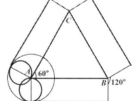

$$N = \frac{2\pi(R+r)}{2\pi \times r} = \frac{R}{r} + 1$$

The total distance the center of the circle travelled is
$$D = 2\pi(R+r)$$

The distance the center of the circle travelled when circle B travels one revolution is
$$d = \frac{2\pi r}{R} \times (R+r).$$

Example 2: The side of equilateral $\triangle ABC$ has length 2π. A circle with radius 1 rolls around the outside of $\triangle ABC$. When the circle first returns to its original position, how many revolutions does it roll?

Solution:

The circle rolls a $180° - 60° = 120°$ arc from point A of AC to point A on AB (1/3 of the circumference of the circle). The circle rolls one revolution from point A of AB to point B on AB.

Total it rolls 4 revolutions.

Theorem 2: Circle A is rolling around a regular n sides polygon with the side length the same as the circumference of the circle without slipping until it returns to its starting point. The number of revolutions the circle A make is $N = n + 1$.

Theorem 3.1: Circle A is rolling around a convex polygon without slipping until it returns to its starting point. If the length of the perimeter of the polygon is n times of the length of the circumference of the circle, the number of revolutions the circle A make is $N = n + 1$.

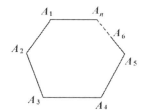

The circle rolls a $(180° - \angle A_1) + (180° - \angle A_2) + ... + (180° - \angle A_n)$
$= 180° \times n - (\angle A_1 + \angle A_2 + ... + \angle A_n) = 180° \times n - 180° \times (n - 2)$
$= 360°$ arc along all vertices.

Theorem 3.2: The distance the center of the circle travels is the sum of the length of the perimeter of the polygon and the length of the circumference of the circle.

Example 3: Circle A of radius 1 is rolling around inside a second circle B of radius 4 without slipping until it returns to its starting point. Find the number of revolutions the circle A makes.

Solution:

The distance D traveled by the centre of the small can be used as a representative distance traveled by it.

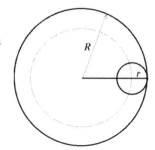

$D = 2\pi (R - r) = = 2\pi (4 - 1) = 6\pi$

The number of revolutions is $\dfrac{6\pi}{2\pi \times 1} = 3$

Theorem 4: Circle A with radius r is rolling around inside a second circle B with radius R without slipping until it returns to its starting point. The number of revolutions the circle A makes is $N = \dfrac{2\pi(R-r)}{2\pi \times r} = \dfrac{R}{r} - 1$.

Theorem 5: A circle with radius r is rolling around inside a triangle with sides a, b, and c without slipping until it returns to its starting point. The distance travelled by the center of the circle is:

The perimeter of triangle $\Delta DEF = m(a + b + c)$

where $m = 1 - \dfrac{pr}{A}$, and $p = \dfrac{1}{2}(a + b + c)$

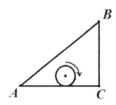 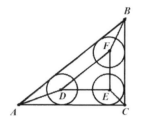

Below shows how we got m:

We know that ΔDEF, of the center of the rolling circle, is similar to ΔABC, so we label its sides ma, mb, mc, for some m and $1 > m > 0$.

The area of ΔABC is $A = \sqrt{p(p-a)(p-b)(p-c)}$ (1)

where $p = \dfrac{1}{2}(a + b + c)$

The area of ΔDEF is $A_1 = \sqrt{mp(mp-ma)(mp-mb)(mp-mc)} = m^2 A$ (2)

Partition ΔABC into three trapezoids of altitude r and ΔDEF, and compute the area of ΔABC in terms of r:

$$[ABC] = [DACE] + [CEFB] + [BFDA] + [DEF]$$

$$= \frac{1}{2}(r)(mb+b) + \frac{1}{2}(r)(ma+a) + \frac{1}{2}(r)(mc+c) + m^2 A$$

$$= \frac{1}{2}(r)(mb+b+ma+a+mc+c) + A = pr(m+1) + m^2 A \qquad (3)$$

We know that (1) = (3). So we have

$$A = pr(m+1) + m^2 A \quad \Rightarrow \quad pr(m+1) + m^2 A - A = 0$$

$$\Rightarrow \quad pr(m+1) + A(m+1)(m-1) = 0.$$

Since $m \neq 0$, $m + 1 \neq 0$. Thus $pr + A(m-1) = 0 \qquad \Rightarrow$

$$m = 1 - \frac{pr}{A}.$$

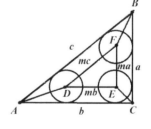

PROBLEMS

Problem 1: A small circle of radius 2 cm is rotating without slipping around a larger circle of radius 10 cm. When the circle first returns to its original position, how many revolutions does the circle roll?

Problem 2: The side of a regular hexagon has length 2π. A circle with radius 1 rolls around the outside of it. When the circle first returns to its original position, how many revolutions does the circle roll?

Problem 3: Circle A with radius 2 is rolling around inside a second circle B with radius 8 without slipping until it returns to its starting point. Find the number of revolutions the circle A makes.

Problem 4: A small circle of radius 2 cm is rotating without slipping around a larger circle of radius 9 cm. If the small circle starts with point A on its circumference in contact with the larger circle, find the exact distance traveled by the centre of the small circle before the point A next comes in contact with the large circle.

Problem 5: (UNL Probe I, 1993) A circle is rolled without slipping, across the top of the other six identical circles to get from the initial position x to the final position y. What is the number of revolutions it must make?

Problem 6: (1993 AMC 12) The sides of $\triangle ABC$ have lengths 6, 8 and 10. A circle with center P and radius 1 rolls around the inside of $\triangle ABC$, always remaining tangent to at least one side of the triangle. When P first returns to its original position, through what distance has P traveled?

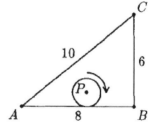

SOLUTIONS:

Problem 1: Solution:

By **Theorem 1,** the number of revolutions the circle A make is

$$N = \frac{2\pi(R+r)}{2\pi \times r} = \frac{R}{r} + 1 = \frac{10}{2} + 1 = 6.$$

Problem 2: Solution:

By **Theorem 2**, the number of revolutions the circle A make is $N = n + 1 = 6 + 1 = 7$.

Problem 3: Solution:

By **Theorem 4,** the number of revolutions the circle A makes is $N = \frac{R}{r} - 1 = \frac{8}{2} - 1 = 4 - 1 = 3$.

Problem 4: Solution:

Method 1:

Since the circumference of the small circle is 4π, the central angle in the large circle between successive points of contact of the point A with the large circle is $\theta = s_1/r = 4\pi/9$.

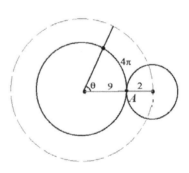

The radius of the circle followed by the centre of the small circle is 11. Thus, the distance traveled by the centre of the small circle before the point A next comes in contact with the large circle is $s_2 = R\theta = (9 + 2)(4\pi/9) = 44\pi/9$.

Method 2:

By the Theorem 1, $d = \frac{2\pi r}{R} \times (R+r) = \frac{2\pi \times 2}{9} \times (9+2) = \frac{44\pi}{9}$.

Problem 5: Solution:

As a circle rolls through one revolution, its center travels a distance equal to the circumference. As the circle moves from position X to position p_1, the center moves a

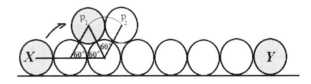

217

distance $2\pi/3$ $(2r) = (4\pi r)/3$. As the circle moves from position p_1 to p_2, the center moves $\pi/3$ $(2r) = (2\pi r)/3$. The total distance traveled by the center of the rolling circle is $2(4\pi r)/3 + 4(2\pi r)/3 = (16\pi r)/3$. Since each revolution is $2\pi r$, the number of revolutions is $16\pi r/3$ divided by $2\pi r$ which is $8/3$.

Problem 6: Solution: 12
We solve this problem by two different methods other than the official solution.

Method 1:

By **Theorem 5:**

The distance $= m(a + b + c)$.
$$m = 1 - \frac{pr}{A} = 1 - \frac{\frac{10+8+6}{2} \times 1}{\frac{8 \times 6}{2}} = 1 - \frac{1}{2} = \frac{1}{2}.$$
So the distance $= m(a + b + c) = (a + b + c)/2 = 12$.

Method 2:

We have $\tan\theta = \dfrac{y}{8}$. By the angle bisector Theorem, we get $\dfrac{8}{y} = \dfrac{10}{6-y}$ $\Rightarrow$ $y = \dfrac{8}{3}$

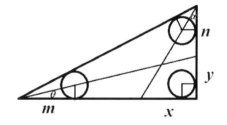

$\tan\theta = \dfrac{r}{m} = \dfrac{1}{m}$ so $\dfrac{1}{m} = \dfrac{\frac{8}{3}}{8}$ $\Rightarrow$ $m = 3$

$\tan\alpha = \dfrac{r}{n} = \dfrac{1}{n}$ and $\dfrac{1}{n} = \dfrac{3}{6}$ $\Rightarrow n = 2$.

Thus the distance travelled $= 8 - (m + 1) + 6 - (n + 1) + 10 - (m + n) = 8 - (3 + 1) + 6 - (2 + 1) + 10 - (3 + 2) = 12$.

Made in the USA
San Bernardino, CA
05 April 2014